This B
Belong

Brenda Crawford

MEMOIRS OF A DRUNKEN PREACHER

RON HENDERSON

Copyright © 2019 by Ron Henderson

All rights reserved.

ISBN: 978-0-578-21792-5

No part of this book may be reproduced in any form or by any electronic or mechanical means, including information storage and retrieval systems, without written permission from the author, except for the use of brief quotations in a book review.

Editing provided by Three Point Author Services (www.threepointauthorservices.com)

Cover Art by Paige1 Media (www.paige1media.com)

I want to thank my four children, who have provided a strong incentive to stay sober. I'd also like to thank the people that never gave up on me—and even the ones that did.

Three Point Author Services have provided structure and their skills to a book that otherwise would have reduced itself to nothing more than kindling for the fire.

I

STARTING OUT ON THE RAGGED EDGE OF LIFE

My first ever memory of life comes from when I was the ripe age of two. I remember being intensely interrogated by three or four adults—a panel of well-meaning people including my stepmother, my grandfather, and my aunt, who were doing all they could to prevent my dad from going to prison. I wasn't sure what they thought they would get from a two-year-old as far as providing some kind of alibi, but that didn't keep them from trying to grill me.

At the time, Dad was in jail, charged with the murder of my mother. My six-year-old brother Bob had found Mom in a pool of blood; she had been beaten, raped and left for dead in our Fort Worth, Texas home. She was 23 years old.

My father had always been an angry drunk. When he was drinking, he hated himself and just about everyone else. It didn't matter who it was—if someone got in his way, they were a potential victim. So, it wasn't surprising that he might be a suspect.

When I was many years older, around the age of 18, my father finally admitted his guilt to me. He also told me that he still loved my mother. I wasn't sure if he told me these things because he wanted to make me feel better—or himself. But one thing was for sure: he hadn't shown my mother much love on the day she died.

There also wasn't much love for his three kids who were left behind. Although Dad got remarried, his second wife left him for allegedly abusing her daughter. I was five at the time.

The task of raising three little kids on his own was more responsibility than Dad was willing to take on, so he looked for alternatives. My younger sister, Sharon, went to live with a distant relative. I was allowed to see her on a regular basis, but it always seemed strange, as if she lived in a different world. The old woman who looked after her—Mom Haughn, as we called her—was deeply religious and cared the world for my sister. Sharon was treated like a queen.

My brother Bob and I were not so lucky. Not long after Sharon was shipped off to Mom Haughn, Dad coerced my grandmother into keeping my brother and me for what he said would be "just one weekend." My grandmother didn't want to take us, but finally she relinquished her will to Dad's manipulations. He took us up to her house in Caney, Kansas, for a visit. Unfortunately, he didn't come back for five whole years.

In those days, living with Grandma felt like a prison sentence to my childish mind. There was never a day that passed when I wasn't reminded that we were unwelcome and unloved in Grandma's house. She would tell me she had been tricked into keeping us, and that she despised Dad for what he had done to her daughter.

In her opinion, the apple didn't fall too far from the tree, and I always felt that she had a deep-seated resentment toward me, perhaps because there was a strong physical resemblance between me and my father. I was what you'd call guilty by association—and I definitely suffered the results of it.

These early years of my life were difficult, and often miserable. I felt sad, unloved, and different from the other kids. I wore dirty, hand-me-down clothes to school. I got a whipping and scolding on a daily basis. Most of the time I suppose I deserved it, but it was still hard to endure.

To compensate for our misery, Bob and I teased my grandmother's youngest daughter, Lana, unmercifully. Our hostility toward her stemmed in part from jealousy. Though she was my aunt, she was younger than me, and she was Grandma's pet, always the most favored. I was the least favored. Bob and I felt like Lana was treated like a little angel while we were the personification of the Devil. So we took out our resentment on her.

In those days, I saw Grandma as the Wicked Witch of the West from *The Wizard of Oz*. By comparison, I saw my father as a combination of John Wayne and Roy Rogers—a real hero. At that young age, I couldn't see how self-consumed he was, or how low my siblings and I ranked on his priority list. I couldn't see the

4

reality that Dad really did not want us. And even if I had been old enough to understand, I still probably would have denied it. What I wanted was to be rescued.

Although my hope in Dad had no basis in reality, I needed someone to gain strength from during the time I lived with my grandmother. I idolized him. I longed for the day that he would come riding over the horizon and rescue Bob and me from the gray hell in which we lived.

On Friday nights, I'd stand outside that little house in Caney, Kansas, under the streetlight, waiting for Dad to come back to break us out of our prison. Each time, after waiting for hours, I would eventually trudge back toward the house with my head down, hoping maybe my knight in shining armor would rescue me the next night.

One night, a car identical to Dad's came around the corner, and I was certain he had come to save me. Elated, I ran out to meet him. But I was wrong—it wasn't him. The car kept going right on past me.

The pain and rejection I felt that night was indescribable. As I walked back to the house with tears running down my cheeks, I told myself that as a father, I would never let my kids feel this degree of pain. Ironically, as my drinking increased later in life, it dawned on me I was duplicating Dad's behavior. It is one of my regrets.

For years, I harbored hate and resentment toward my grandmother for the way she treated my brother Bob and me. As time took its course, I was eventually able to understand things better from her perspective. She had suffered the loss of a beloved daughter—my mother. Then Dad successfully manipulated the court system by only doing six months in jail for murder. Then he manipulated her into raising his two sons. Her husband, my grandfather, had died in his bed—drunk. In addition, she lived in abject poverty, and my brother and I only compounded the problem.

As difficult as my early childhood was at times, I am grateful to have had the companionship of my brother Bob who was four years older than me, and my Uncle John, three years older. Bob especially was influential on me. We remained close until his death two years ago. In a weird way, Bob was kind of like a dad to me since my real Dad was AWOL.

Because of Bob and Uncle John, I have some fond memories from the time I lived in that household. And looking back, I realize now that Grandma did the best she could with the limited hand that was dealt to her.

Grandma had remarried a kind Native American man named Georgie. He hauled trash for five dollars a month per household to help make ends meet. Having my brother and me around meant having two more mouths to feed, making a total of seven people in the family. I felt like a stray dog that had wandered up to the house and mooched a place to stay.

Over time, of course, we can get attached to strays, and there were times that I did feel loved. And Georgie was an important source of that love.

Georgie was a compassionate soul. I could read in his eyes the sorrow he felt for Bob and me when Grandma unleashed one of her venomous tirades. Although he never stood up to her, he demonstrated kindness to us by allowing us to go on fishing trips to the river. Since we were not ardent fishermen, we always swam and had mud ball fights instead. He was patient, gentle, and kind in every way imaginable.

I also remember clearly how Georgie played the fiddle—one of my favorite memories of him. It was common for him to have a few of his friends over to the house on Saturday night to pick and grin. Speaking of grinning, Georgie didn't have many teeth but when he smiled, his entire face lit up. He taught me that simplicity is the essence of life. He never received an education, never owned a home to my knowledge, and never had an expensive car, but he was one of the simplest, happiest men I have ever known.

Life Lesson #1: Happiness is found in the simple things, like fishing or playing the fiddle.

ALTHOUGH MY EARLY life certainly had some painful memories, it was also filled with activities and events that would make any little kid envious. One of the advantages of helping Grandpa Georgie with his trash hauling business was riding in the back of his truck. Georgie drove a '51 Ford he had painted green with a brush. Bob, Uncle John, and I rode in the back of his truck along with the trash, in search of any form of entertainment that would add a little excitement and adventure to the otherwise mundane task of hauling other people's garbage.

Georgie drove his pickup so slowly that if he'd gone any slower, we would've been moving backwards. So we'd jump out of the back of the truck and run, trying to keep up. Before our last ounce of energy was spent, we'd lunge for the tailgate, climb back in, and imagine that we'd won first place in the Boston Marathon. Most of the time, that approach seemed to work quite well. Occasionally my devious brother would beat my hands as I was trying to get back in, and I'd have to walk the long, lonely, dusty road to the dump and try to slip back into the group without being noticed.

When we got to the dump, we would immediately get to work. What other people deemed as trash, we defined as treasure, and we'd sift through the discarded garbage, dirty diapers and old food, ignoring the gagging odor, seeing ourselves as miners hunting for gold. Often, we'd find something that we could use. And as poor as we were, finding a functional toy was like a trip to Toys R Us. The only downside to those exciting shopping sprees was when neighborhood kids came to our house and recognized the toys that used to be theirs before they threw them away. I learned to keep my stash well hidden.

My brother quickly became an entrepreneurial type. We would find junk bikes at the dump and haul them home. Bob would then make some basic repairs and resell the good-as-new bikes for a sizable profit (five, maybe six dollars). In a few years, we gained the reputation as the premier Bicycle Salvage Yard of

Caney, Kansas. I remember an older gentleman from Dewey, Oklahoma, would make his monthly visit to barter and haggle with my brother over miscellaneous items.

We continually attracted a steady flow of buddies who needed parts for their bikes. The irony was that sometimes Bob sold them a wheel off of the same bicycle which they had thrown away and we had picked up at the dump. Maybe my brother found his calling at this young age, because for thirty-plus years, he owned and operated a classic car salvage yard, twenty miles from where he started fifty years earlier.

Among our peers, we were considered poor white trash, but we were popular, well-liked white trash. All in all, we learned to adapt to make the best out of a not-so-good situation.

Life Lesson #2: Your attitude toward your circumstances shapes your destiny, not the circumstances themselves.

II

WILD CAR CHASES AND MOTORCYCLE RACES

WE LIVED with Grandma and Grandpa Georgie until I was around ten years old. Dad eventually decided to come back and get us, much to my surprise—and probably everyone else's too. I had given up on the possibility of him ever returning, let alone living with him again. By that time, I had quit waiting at the corner for him to rescue me.

But when he came to get us and we moved back to North Texas, I conveniently forgot all about the fact that a one-weekend stay had turned into five years. He was my hero once again.

On good days, Dad modeled how to work hard and taught us how to turn a mundane work environment into a carnival. He had a solid reputation as the go-to guy when it came to gags and games in the workplace.

He would make semi-nonlethal acetylene bombs that sounded like a nuclear explosion. After the bomb went off, he joined everyone else in looking for the origin of the explosion. When the police arrived, he would make suggestions as to the possible source of the noise. Other times, he would act as though he didn't hear the noise the officer was describing.

His work ethic in his earlier days was unparalleled. I witnessed him straightening frames on damaged cars, sweat dripping down his face, tools flying everywhere, in his obsessive determination to get everything just right. His focus was uninterrupted. His drive was like that of a rat on methamphetamines.

At this time, Dad was single—a tall, handsome, charismatic, heavy-drinking, woman-chasing hombre. On weekends he would throw us a handful of cash and head to the bar. I don't ever remember going grocery shopping; soda pop and hamburgers were our steady diet. It couldn't have been better.

It was also common practice for him to provide us with a steady flow of go-carts, Cushman Motor Scooters, and dirt bikes. Dad took out loans to buy these things. He allowed me to drive back and forth to school years before I was even eligible to get a legal driver's license—the only kid in junior high with such a privilege.

I would have preferred his guidance and time, of course. But I was still a kid, and this stuff worked as a substitute for a while. It wasn't until I was around 18 that I started to accept the reality of all of his shortcomings.

In other words, Dad did have a few interesting and even admirable qualities. Like most people, he had his good traits as well as bad ones.

Over the years, I have rarely—if ever—met anyone who was all good or all bad. For the most part, I make it a habit to accentuate their strengths and minimize their weaknesses. With some people, however, it's sometimes a little harder to see their strengths.

Life Lesson #3: Make it a habit to accentuate people's strengths and minimize their weaknesses. Rarely is anyone all good or all bad.

But some things never seemed to change—including Dad's dysfunctional romantic relationships. And this took a toll on my siblings and me.

Dad's third marriage was an adjustment for us all, including his new wife. She had never been blessed with children of her own. So, as you might imagine, it was almost cruel to introduce her to two little boys who often acted like untamed animals.

Before their marriage, Dad told Maureen he was going to ship us back to Kansas at the end of the summer. Even back then, as young as I was, this statement felt to me like a trick to get her to marry him. In Dad's own way, perhaps he was trying do the best he could for his two unmanageable sons, but it was obvious that she had no idea what she was in for.

Dad and his new wife were polar opposites. He was a hard-drinking womanizer, while she was a naïve, young, inhibited Catholic girl. They represented the picture-perfect odd couple. And again, my brother and I found ourselves living in a household with another woman who detested our presence. Dad had sold her a false bill of goods; he never did ship us back to Kansas. It was an unpleasant, awkward situation.

For these reasons and others, I wanted to escape from the pain of reality. By the time I was a teenager, I had found a solution to all of my problems. It conveniently made all of the fear, rejection, and justified feelings of abandonment disappear. I'm talking, of course, about alcohol.

My addiction started with what seemed like an ingenious scheme at the time: one night I stole a fifth of whiskey from Dad. He always had an ample supply, and besides, the next day he wouldn't remember it was gone anyway.

A few close friends and I chugged the whiskey in record time. For the first time in my life, I finally felt whole and complete. It seemed as if all my huge insecurities shrunk down to the size of a speck of dust, all thanks to the warmth of the cheap whiskey. I felt large and in charge, confident and outgoing. All of a sudden, I was funny, wild, and kind of cute, all at the same time. I liked the new me!

The events that followed were a blur, and I have no memory of what happened until I woke up in the Johnson County jail in Cleburne, Texas the next morning. I didn't know where I was or how I got there. But I was of the firm conviction that whatever had happened, it would be a really good idea for me to exit that jail as quickly as possible, before my dad found out I was there. I didn't expect him to be too impressed with his youngest son's behavior. Unfortunately, since this was my first stint in jail, I wasn't a well-trained escape artist. I paced the jail cell, stuck, until Dad came and got me out.

As I walked out into the lobby, I was surprised at his response. I had expected threats, anger, and harsh discipline—but there was none of that. Instead, I could see hurt and disappointment in his eyes. It was as if his son was drifting further and further away from shore, and there was nothing he could do about it. He looked hopeless, as if I was going away to a strange land, and he wasn't sure whether I would ever return. In an odd way, his presence communicated fear and disappointment.

But somehow, I had no regrets.

Regardless of Dad's disappointment with me, I had fallen in love with the way alcohol made me feel. That first experience was the beginning of a long-lasting, messy relationship with booze. So what if I was grounded for a few weeks when I got caught? The good that the whiskey had provided far outweighed the bad. I had fallen in love with a power greater than myself. It could turn a weak, feeble kid into a cross between King Kong and Godzilla all in one small body.

The following Monday, when I got to school, I wanted to know what happened that blissful night I lost my memory due to my first alcohol-induced blackout. I knew I'd had a lot of fun; I just couldn't remember exactly how much.

Danny, my drinking colleague said, "You don't remember? You

were great! You were dancing on the table at the Dairy Queen, and the manager told you to get off or he was going to call the police. Then you said, 'Hey, I'm not hurting anybody. I just want to dance.'"

I said, "Danny, that's a big lie. I don't even know how to dance!"

Danny's responded, "I didn't say you were a good dancer, but you *were* dancing on the table!"

It seemed I had found a savior that could deliver me from all of my troubles. My friends gave me undue recognition and respect for my drunken, crazy behavior. For a lowly little eighth grader riddled with fear and insecurity, it was quite a sense of accomplishment—I felt I had discovered my identity. I had found a medication that took away the emptiness. And although it was only temporary, it took away all the pain that I felt inside.

Life Lesson #4: Self-medication works—but only temporarily.

It wasn't long before I had started to drink regularly and get into trouble. At one point, I had a short-lived career at a local mechanic's garage, pumping gas and taking care of other chores. One Saturday morning the owner, Robert, informed me that he had to go to town to take care of some errands. I was in charge! It was kind of scary, but I accepted the challenge.

What Robert hadn't realized was that I was nursing a major hangover that morning. In an effort to lessen the pain of an agonizing headache, I went into the bathroom, locked the door, and proceeded to sleep off my hangover. It seemed like a brilliant idea at the time—I'd take a quick nap and upon waking, I'd feel refreshed and ready to perform my usual duties at an optimum level.

I never gave one moment's thought to the idea that any customers might need gas while I was sleeping. Unfortunately for me, the next sound I heard was the owner beating loudly on the door, waking me from a peaceful state of slumber. Robert was furious that I had been so irresponsible. He proceeded to inform me that my brief tenure with him was over.

In other words—I was fired.

As I was walking away, Robert yelled across the drive, "Hey, boy, your dad was paying me to keep you employed here in hopes that you might stay out of trouble and learn some responsibility!" As I kept walking, he threw one more jab my way: "You ain't no good, boy, and you never will be!"

I was thinking to myself, he might just be right. If I was working for a guy and it wasn't costing him anything—if he was making money on the deal, yet he'd just fired me—then the gentlemen might have swerved into some truth about me. In my heart, I felt Robert was right. I wasn't any good. But salvation in a bottle would come shortly. I would drink to numb the pain.

Of course, that wasn't the only time in my young life that I made poor decisions because of my shame, pain, and drinking.

Even with all of the amenities that came with being the only eighth grader who rode his motorcycle to school, that notoriety wasn't quite enough for me. Sometimes when we're on a quest to be cool and garner attention, we are capable of doing some illogical, irrational, and just plain stupid stunts. Add in an addiction to adrenaline highs, and things can get even crazier.

One summer night, several months after getting fired, I was cruising around on my Suzuki 120cc when I spotted our 1966 Ford Galaxy behind that very same garage. My curiosity got the best of me, so I wheeled my bike around and proceeded to investigate the situation. I couldn't believe my eyes—Robert had left the keys in the car! It was an opportunity that many may dream about, but only a few get to live out.

I wasn't drunk that night, but I was in the mood to cause some trouble. It seemed like the intelligent thing to do was to hide my bike in the bushes and go riding in style! Within fifteen minutes, I had four of my best friends in the car with me. The tunes were cranking (as much as an AM radio with factory speakers would crank), and we were rolling by the park where everybody hung out.

My head hardly reached above the window opening in the door, but I felt cool to the core, waving at my friends—especially the girls. I assumed that most of them had been brought to the park by their parents. But not me! I was driving to the park!

As we rolled past, I sat as high as I could in the seat to make sure everyone noticed me. I waved and winked like a rock star would to his fans at a concert. For a few moments, I was the coolest person I had ever known. No one asked for my autograph, but I knew they wanted it. As Andy Warhol said, "We all have our fifteen minutes of fame."

Unfortunately, my personal fifteen minutes were about to come to a screeching halt.

As I peered at the rearview mirror, I thought to myself, "Who is the asshole tailgating me?" I realized it was a '65 Ford pickup, similar to the one my dad drove. No... it wasn't similar to the truck my dad drove; it *was* the one he drove—with him in it. He was following his own car as it was being driven, without permission, by his son and a bunch of his son's little punk buddies!

The logical thing for Dad to do was pull us over, get out of the car, and give me an ass-whooping in front of my friends, plus all of the girls in my fan club. And I dreaded it. So without giving any other options a lot of thought, I accelerated the car full throttle. My plan was to ditch Dad, who was in hot pursuit. Then I'd return his car to the garage, get back on my motorcycle and eventually stroll in the front door, pretending that nothing had happened. At the time, it seemed like a sensible thing to do.

The race was on! We were sliding around corners on the dirt roads like cops and robbers. Dad had taught me to drive his '51 Ford with a Mustang 289 cubic-inch motor, while we drank beer on the country roads near Cleburne, Texas. I knew how to take the corners, but I had never questioned the fact that he was the better driver.

All I can say is, this time around I just got lucky. As I turned a corner, the car slid sideways, and I ended up in a stranger's driveway. I hit the lights and ordered my friends to duck. Dad raced right past us. So far, the plan was working brilliantly.

I explained to my friends that my life was in danger and that they must get out of the car and walk back to the park. They understood; well, everybody except Danny Carper. Danny had broken his leg in a motorcycle wreck and was still on crutches. I was hoping that *someday* he would understand. After I threatened to break his other leg if he didn't get out, Danny reluctantly decided it was his time to walk. At that particular moment, I was thinking of my ass, not his leg.

As I made that long journey back to the mechanic's garage, I could only imagine the final outcome, my final demise. Would the S.W.A.T. team be there, hiding in the trees, or did Dad have enough time to hire some thugs from the hood to slap me around and rough me up a little? Another possibility: he didn't know it had been me, and I would get back on my bike and plead the Fifth Amendment when interrogated.

When I got back to the shop, my worst nightmare had come true. My motorcycle was gone; Dad had loaded it into the back of his truck and was holding it as evidence. Not trusting my reasoning power anymore, I decided to walk back instead of driving his car. After all, it was his—who gave me the right to drive it?

I didn't know how the story was going to end, but I knew it was not going to be pretty. While I didn't think I would actually be charged with grand theft auto and spend ten to twenty years in prison, I felt sure my trial and conviction would be quick and painful.

As I trudged the three or four miles home along the streets of Cleburne, a long and scary trip in light of what was sure to come, my life seemed to pass before my eyes. I felt as though I was on my journey to the electric chair. I then realized that driving the car home would have been better; the seemingly endless wait for my conviction would have come faster.

While I was walking, Dad had been working on his game plan in the front seat of his truck while chugging cheap whiskey. He was not always a fun guy to be around, even when he was sober. And when he was mad, mean, and drunk, I had developed the art of avoiding him altogether. Tonight, however, avoidance was not an option.

I had one last trick in my bag. My plan was to slither past Dad like a grass snake in the lawn, rush in the house, take off my clothes, jump into bed and do the ole' possum trick and play like I was either dead or asleep. Being the gentle, kind person that he was about one percent of the time, maybe there was a slim chance he wouldn't want to disturb me out of a deep sleep. It would only give me a temporary stay of execution, but after the whiskey wore off, maybe his sentence would be more lenient.

Wrong! I had hardly enough time to get undressed before he

came storming into my room. I won't bore you with the mundane details of the beating I got. Suffice it to say that for several days after the famous car chase, my ass felt and looked like raw hamburger. And just in case there was a chance of me forgetting that horrendous night, all I had to do was glance at the ceiling of my bedroom to see the blood splatters from his stern style of discipline. My brother had already left home due to Dad's style of leadership. If he would have been at home that night, Bob would have intervened on his little brother's behalf, just as he had on many other occasions.

Apparently, Dad had never heard of things like the time-out corner, or deep-breathing exercises before reacting. In my heart, I felt a lingering feeling that I was no good—rotten to the core. That same year, I discovered how stolen whiskey from Dad could make that sense of inferiority temporarily go away.

For the rational person, the consequences of taking Dad's car would have been a good lesson. A rational person would have decided to never steal one of Dad's cars again. But I failed to meet the criteria for being rational.

Some of us are slow learners. Real slow. On another occasion, I took Dad's '61 Chevy hardtop for a joyride. This time, he didn't actually catch me, and the car was back in its parking place before he ever got home. But somehow, he instinctively knew it had been moved, even though I'd been careful to put it back in its proper place. He started questioning me about where I had taken his car, and I denied everything until he lifted the hood and firmly placed my hand on the top of the hot radiator.

At that point, my alibi fell apart, and it felt like my hand did too. I have made a lot of mistakes over the past six decades, but I never made the mistake of driving one of his vehicles ever again without permission. Between a bleeding ass and a scalded hand, it just seemed like it wasn't worth it anymore.

Some might think Dad's style of discipline was a bit abusive and extreme. I would agree. Sometimes he would get a certain look in his eyes, and I knew that if I pushed beyond that point, he could snap, and the outcome wouldn't be pretty. In a crude way, I learned an element of respect for authority figures.

That lesson seems to be missing in today's world. There is a lack of respect for authority in schools, at work, at home, and most definitely it's missing toward law enforcement officials. Being buddies with our kids has taken precedence over respect and honor.

Life Lesson #5: Acquiescing to authority figures is usually the best idea. But if the judicial system is corrupt, stay away from it.

Around eighth grade, Dad bought me another motorcycle. What a wild, dangerous combination—a drunken kid on a motorcycle. When things got a little slow in my life, I just got drunk and rode down the wrong side of the street with the headlights off, strictly for the adrenaline rush and attention.

Over the course of my life, a few folks have accused me of having a death wish. Maybe there already was lodged within me, at that young age, a deep-seated hope that death might be better than life. If we have never received the gift of life from our creator, then it's easy for us to think death might be superior to life.

Around this time of experimenting with alcohol and wild driving experiences, I also—not surprisingly—had more clashes with the law.

After a school dance one Saturday night, Officer Johnny Johnson detected my unstable, drunken driving habits. By the time he was able to turn his police cruiser around and flip his lights on, I was already well ahead of him. I knew I didn't have a chance to lose him on the open road, so instead I headed to a familiar neighborhood.

There were probably two reasons why he never caught me that night. My theory is that, first of all, a smaller motorcycle can maneuver around corners more easily than a big car. Secondly, I just didn't care. Johnny probably had a family who needed and cared for him, and he probably felt the same way about them. I didn't feel that way; I had nothing to lose.

Whatever the case, I slid around several corners, then pulled between two parked cars in a driveway. Johnny sped right by, not seeing me. He went back to the dance and questioned some friends of mine, who didn't give him the answers he wanted. Meanwhile, with the taste of alcohol on my lips and the adrenaline rush of living on the edge, I had found a new love!

I have told my kids I want this poem to be the epitaph on my tombstone. It was written by Hunter S. Thompson, in his book *Hell's Angels: A Strange and Terrible Saga:*

. . .

Life should not be a journey to the grave
  With the intention of arriving
  Safely in a pretty and well-preserved body,
  But rather to skid in broadside in a cloud of smoke,
  Thoroughly used up,
  Totally worn out,
  And loudly proclaiming,
  "Wow!
  What a ride!"

We have two options, we can take the safe and secure route as we travel through life or we can overcome our fears, take calculated risks and find fulfillment. Within the heart of every man, I believe there is an innate desire to be a part of something far bigger than himself—a cause big enough and noble enough that he is willing to devote his life and even sacrifice his life for it, if need be. If we fail to absorb ourselves in something greater than ourselves, we are dissatisfied in a way that we find hard to resolve. So, we try to escape by consuming ourselves with video games, reality TV, overindulgence in sports, adventure-seeking behavior, or medicating our minds with intoxicating beverages and drugs.

In reality, we long to be crusaders—heroes and conquerors of some kind. But without a commitment to a higher purpose, we slowly develop an addiction to mediocrity. Jesus said, "If any man wishes to be my disciple, let him take up his cross and follow me. If any man wishes to save his life, let him lose it" (Matthew 16:24). He meant we should lose it in a legacy that outlives ourselves.

By the way, I quit riding my motorcycle drunk, with the headlights off, on the wrong side of the street, when I got sober. But God forbid that I lose my passion for life and bow to the fear of failure. I still drive fast sometimes. I still take risks. That's what it means to be alive.

Life Lesson #6: Don't be afraid to take risks—but take calculated risks, instead of foolish ones.

III

A FAILED ATTEMPT TO FULFILL A DEATH WISH

Life seemed to trickle on for the next three years. We lived on the ragged edge of life. Fighting with Dad, drinking hard, and getting kicked out of school became my routine behavior.

One day, the vice principal of my high school summed up my life both clearly and painfully. I had already been kicked out of school over twenty times, usually for petty stuff like pulling the fire alarm and fighting. This time, Mr. Hopper called me to his office for another disciplinary matter. As I sat down, he said to me, "Ronnie, I have been in education for over twenty years, so I think I can speak with some accuracy on the subject we are going to discuss." I congratulated him on a long and successful career.

Unamused, he went on to say, "I have seen guys like you before, and I predict that by the time you're eighteen, you will either be in a mental institution or in prison. So, here's the deal. In Texas, as you might know, you can't legally quit school at your age. However, if you'll just leave today and not come back, you'll never be reported to the authorities. It will be our little secret, and you'll be doing us both a favor."

Although accepting the offer would have been my first choice, I knew Dad wouldn't agree with the plan. So I declined Mr. Hopper's invitation. But as I walked out of his office, in my heart I knew he was right. I didn't belong in school.

From that point forward, it seemed that all I had to do was drop my pencil, and I was out the school door for a few days. Most of the time, of course, I did much worse than just drop my pencil. Sometimes I would simply tell the truth—that I had played hooky for a day—and Vice Principal Hopper would kick me out for three more days, a more than fair deal. I didn't want to be there, and I knew the school staff were relieved when I wasn't, so it seemed like a win-win deal. And I couldn't forget his haunting forecast of my future.

Around that same time, our family was asked to leave the second trailer park in Cleburne. The owner said I was creating too much of a disturbance—throwing lawn furniture in the swimming pool, stealing eight-track cassettes from cars, walking into the wrong trailer house drunk, throwing eggs and fruit at cars as they passed by, and other disruptive behaviors. We hear about "trailer trash," but what is it called if you are even below trailer trash status?

I continued my educational process for one more year, until the principal of the high school in Joshua, Texas came to a similar conclusion as Mr. Hopper did. The principal informed me that he was tired of me causing trouble, and would I please clean out my locker and never come back? He politely informed me that I was a troublemaker, and he was done trying to work with me.

At this point, I had allowed others in my life to shape my destiny. It felt like my life was an out-of-control train, just waiting for the end to come.

Life Lesson #7: Don't let other people shape your destiny.

It seems that there are some members of the human race who are so consumed with shame, that we subconsciously feel unworthy of the gift of life. It would explain why some people have such a morbid outlook on life, having the belief that we are wasting people's time, space, and air. I know what that feels like.

By the time I was sixteen, I felt like I was destined to be a lifetime loser. I am reminded of that old song by Meatloaf, *Life Is a Lemon and I Want My Money Back*. That's pretty much the way I felt. So in the fall of 1970, I faced the grim reality that it was time to clean out my locker and see if there was a better game in the next life.

One evening, before departing for another night of guzzling cheap wine and listening to loud music, I remember Dad saying, "Now don't go out and get drunk, you little bastard!" As I left the house, I asked myself, *Did I hear him say, 'Now go out and get drunk, you little bastard?' Yeah, that's what he said. If he didn't say it exactly that way, that's probably what he meant.*

Later that night, I found myself once again drunk, out of friends, and out of money. However, my memory of what Dad said slowly began to come back. He had told me *not* to get drunk!

Rather than suffer his wrath from coming home drunk one more time and having to face a big fight, I came up with another one of my ingenious plans. I felt the most logical thing to do was to quietly sneak in the back door of our trailer house, and from there I would slither like a snake down the hall and into my bedroom. The next day, when Dad asked me what time I got home, I would politely tell him that he was asleep on the sofa when I got in, and I didn't want to wake him. It seemed like a perfect idea.

The only thing I hadn't calculated into my plan was that my younger sister's bedroom was directly across the hall from the back door. When Sharon saw a long, skinny arm reaching into the house, she let out a bloodcurdling scream that woke up half of the people in the trailer park.

Oops!

I knew it was late, and I knew I was drunk, but my mind was of course still working, churning out bright ideas that were not so bright after all. I quickly closed the door, ran briskly into the field behind the trailer, and lay down to get some much-needed rest. After all the dust settled, I would just walk right in the front door, completely sober.

At that point, I would demand to know what all the commotion had been about. As soon as they told me about the attempted burglary, I would insist on apprehending the villain. If I couldn't find him, at least I would get an honorable mention for trying, and I could go peacefully to bed.

In retrospect, it would have been a good idea to get a second opinion on my so-called brilliant plan.

Life Lesson #8: As "ingenious" ideas emerge, a second opinion can often be beneficial.

Looking back, I am still astounded at my stupidity! As I lay quietly on my back in the field, it seemed at first that all was going to plan. Lights came on all around the trailer park. Some of the neighbors wanted to know what the commotion was about. I heard Dad say that our family had just been victims of an attempted burglary.

After lying in the weeds for what seemed like an eternity, I decided it was time to make my entrance. All was going well—until I got up and stumbled into the house.

As I walked in, Dad said in a thundering voice, "Aha, it was you, you little bastard, and you're drunk!"

Needless to say, he wasn't impressed with my performance that night. My best-laid plans had failed again. I realized that the events of that evening pretty much summed up the way I managed my entire life. Dad reminded me what a disgraceful piece of human debris I was, and I agreed with him.

If we suspect that we have no self-worth, and others in our life seem to support that belief, we begin to believe it on a deeper level. And we proceed to act all the more like we are losers.

As I walked down the hallway after having been chewed out by Dad, I did a brief review of how I felt about myself and how others felt about me. I thought back to the conversations with those well-meaning educators who had predicted my future. I felt like a first-class misfit.

Then I had an idea. I didn't think Dad would mind if I were to borrow one of his double-edged razor blades and make a quiet exit. I went back to my bedroom and slashed my wrist.

Dad later discovered my limp body lying in a pool of blood. He loved me enough to pick me up and rush me to the hospital. I received eighteen stitches in my left wrist.

My body healed, but I was still emotionally and spiritually sick. Inside I was a vacant vessel, drifting at sea without a rudder. I just wanted to quit.

I see now that even when I wasn't very likable, God was still there, protecting and guiding me. In those days, however, I knew nothing about the love of God. I continued to slide down that slippery slope of emptiness and loneliness, always feeling like an outsider.

Life Lesson #9: Tough times are only temporary, don't quit.

WHEN I WAS SEVENTEEN, I moved away from Dad because of his perverted, abusive behavior with my sister, Sharon. While I can't remember how I first learned about the abuse, I remember I was still a teenager when I found out about it. I didn't know how to help Sharon properly. I could barely help myself, let alone anyone else.

The truth is, Dad was overpowering and intimidating. I don't believe Sharon would have been able to stop him from abusing her on her own. From what she told me later in life, the adults she did seek help from placed the blame on her, not Dad

All I knew was that I couldn't take seeing it anymore. I was just so disgusted by it all. I packed my duffle bag, and as I walked toward the door to leave, I told Dad that I would never live in the same household with him again. Separating myself from him was the right thing to do—with the exception of leaving my sister alone with his barbaric, sick behavior. I have asked her to forgive me several times over, and she has done so. We both agree his behavior wasn't either of our faults. But I still regret that I didn't find a way to stay and support Sharon. All I can say to anyone that might be victim of abuse, is to share your story with trusted friend, get professional help, above all don't bottle it up!

Instead, I did the only thing I could think of. I hitchhiked back to Kansas and asked Grandma if she would let me stay with her. She reluctantly consented; her feelings toward me hadn't changed much, but I just had no other place to go.

I chose not to tell Grandma why I left Texas. She had enough reasons to hate Dad, and I didn't think I needed to throw any more into the mix. An hour after I arrived, I overheard her talking to the next-door neighbor as they sat on the front porch. She told the neighbor how much she despised the idea of me being there. She said I had a defiant, rebellious attitude.

I could have used that as an opportunity to look inward to see if there was any truth to her remarks. Instead, I took the self-pity route and decided to feel sorry for myself. It would have been more beneficial to be honest with myself.

Life Lesson #10: If others make an observation about you, look within to see if there is any kernel of truth to it.

I STAYED with Grandma because I had no other place to go. I'd like to say that we got along great because I changed my attitude, but that wouldn't be true. I was a wreck, just waiting for a disaster to happen. Grandma barely tolerated my drunken behavior as I stumbled into the house late at night, knocking over lamps or tripping on the dog.

She did the best she could to extend love and support, with very little from me in return. I had an obsession with myself—not because I felt great, but because I felt so insignificant. Nonetheless, it was still a form of self-absorption. And my addiction to drinking only made things worse.

In the beginning, addiction is typically characterized by fun and frivolity. In most cases, we drink because we like the way it makes us feel. We enjoy the comfort it provides in social settings; we want to feel accepted in a group that just wants to have fun. In the early stages of addiction, we are still able to function adequately on the job. Our drinking hasn't yet created too many conflicts at home, with law enforcement, or at our place of employment.

However, the curve moves downward as our addiction increases. Our drinking changes from a want to a need. The balance between pain and pleasure begins to shift in pain's favor. The negative aspects of our addiction begin to pull ahead, and if we continue, pain will not only take the lead but start doing laps around the pleasure. And in some cases, the end is death.

At this stage, I was in denial about the reality of my drinking addiction. What money I made, I spent on alcohol. I would drink until I passed out or ran out of money, whichever came first.

This same year I finally quit school for good, instead of waiting to be kicked out. I got a job in an auto body shop, sanding cars during the day and sleeping with the boss's wife at night. Some of my buddies came by the shop on a bright, sunshiny day to tell me they were skipping school and heading to State Lake to celebrate their graduation. Although I wasn't graduating, I decided to celebrate with them anyway. I was always ready for a party, and I didn't have anything better to do besides work, so I dropped my sanding block, walked off the job and left with my friends. The event turned into a festive occasion, with cold beer flowing and loud music blaring.

We were all having a great time—until the game warden decided to take one of our friends to jail on a drunk in public charge. I proceeded to inform him that he would not be taking my friend to jail; I wasn't going to allow it, and furthermore, he didn't have the authority since he was just a game warden. He let me know that he was not only taking Marshall to jail, but I was going too.

I conceded I might have been wrong, so as well as any 17-year old drunk could, I politely stated, "Well, I stand corrected. Maybe you will be taking him to jail, but there is no way I am going, and you can't make me!" I then swam out to the tower, a platform fifty yards off shore, and started calling him names and taunting him. The officer left with my friend, and my peers hailed me as a hero.

One of the characteristics of a shame-based life is that on the surface, we project an invincible image full of bravado. But on the inside, we are weak and frail, governed by a thousand different forms of fear. We try to act cool, confident, and secure, while we are anything but. I believed in my heart that if anybody knew the real Ron, they wouldn't like me. So, I tried to be somebody I wasn't.

That night, all alone, I lay in bed afraid of what might happen. My friends weren't there, and I was scared. Within my heart was a trembling little kid that few people ever got to know.

The next day, the sheriff came to the house during a family reunion, bringing with him a warrant. He arrested me for being drunk in public and resisting arrest. I learned that the game warden had more authority than I had realized.

Of course, it wasn't to be my last brush with the law. But in the meantime, I started contemplating my options.

My brother told me he would give me two hundred dollars if I would graduate from high school. He never honored his commitment, but the trick worked. I had been out of school for a year, and I realized that there didn't seem to be much of a future for me in washing dishes and sanding cars. But I would be stuck doing this kind of work for the rest of my life unless I got a better education. So, I enrolled back in school.

I completed my junior year with one of the lowest grade point averages in the history of the school. My senior year started off similarly to the way the rest of my life had gone—rough and rocky. Out of the goodness of her heart, my stepmother sent money for my class ring. I thought it would be a better investment to buy Boones Farm Wine with the money.

As part of the celebration, my buddy Gene and I headed to Bartlesville, Oklahoma, where the girls were prettier than the ones Kansas had to offer. Incidentally, we didn't find any pretty girls who wanted to be associated with the likes of us. A girl would need to have the IQ of a grapefruit in order for that to happen. But youth is nothing if not optimistic.

On our way back to Kansas, driving with one eye closed to avoid double vision from all the drinking, I hit a parked car on the side of the Highway 75. We must have been going at least 50–55 miles per hour when I hit the parked car head on. Miraculously, neither Gene nor I sustained any head injuries. Some might say our drunk, limp bodies kept us from harm. Personally, I feel it must have been the grace of God at work.

It seemed like only a few minutes passed before the Highway Patrol arrived. The officer inquired after our well-being, and when he determined there were no serious injuries, he let us know we were going to jail. Gene was arrested for an outstanding warrant.

While the officer was in his patrol car, I found a hunting knife that Gene had stuffed under his seat. My intention was to throw it in the weeds before the officer searched us. But my timing was a little off. He ordered us to get out of the car before I could toss the knife. When he asked if we had any weapons, we said no. He proceeded to pat us down. Then he found the knife. He assumed I was preparing to stab him, and he lost any remaining sense of kindness. He started tossing us around like hardened criminals, rapists, or serial murders instead of a couple of drunk teenagers.

Through the intervention of my older brother and my grandmother, I was given only a small fine and released from jail in a few days. Close friends began to hint that I might have a drinking problem.

I refused to agree with them. To me, alcohol wasn't my problem; it was my solution. It made me feel complete. When I was under the influence, I felt confident and bold. To take my alcohol away would be like stealing Popeye's spinach, or handing Superman kryptonite. Although others may have accurately identified the problem, I couldn't imagine what the solution was.

Eventually, though, drinking became less satisfying. The shine of that lifestyle began to wear off. I found myself growing tired of being around my drinking buddies, and other things began to happen as well that made me rethink my past decisions.

I was dating a girl named Suzie at this time. Of all the relationships I had been in, she was one of the few women I genuinely cared for. She was a decent girl with standards far above mine. She was attracted to me, but her dad, who was also my boxing coach, wasn't. He informed her that I drank too much and that I had bad blood in me, refusing to let me date her anymore. I couldn't exactly blame him.

Looking back now, I can remember being introduced to sniffing gasoline and glue as a mere seventh grader in Mineral Wells, Texas. These cheap, accessible substances took me to places I had never been before. One of my friends never came back. Then I moved into using alcohol and drugs when I was in eighth grade, in Cleburne, Texas. While the chemicals and alcohol gave me temporary relief, within a few hours I was back to being the same, lonely mess that I was before getting high.

Through it all, I kept searching for meaning and purpose in life. But nothing really worked. So as I approached my upper teens, I directed my efforts toward being more responsible.

After my junior year in high school, my lifestyle finally started to change a little. I wasn't drinking as much, because it didn't bring the same, easy experiences it once had. But I wasn't any happier either. My love affair with alcohol had left me empty, but I didn't know that the answer was life—and God.

I went through the motions. I moved out of my grandmother's house and found a garage apartment, then took a job at the box factory during my senior year of high school. I was making about thirty dollars a week. Rent for my garage apartment was fourteen dollars. Times were tough, but I found a way of surviving. It wasn't easy.

For example, on payday one time, I decided to spend beyond my means—I bought a *Webster's Dictionary* at Baker's Drug Store for six dollars. By the time I got home, I was feeling a pending sense of doom and fear for spending beyond my budget. I recall lying on my bed crying, wondering how I would pay rent and afford gas for my car back and forth to school and work.

Somehow, though, the rent got paid, and I still have the dictionary today. Sometimes we tend to take small issues and unknowingly maximize their size, worrying over them for no purpose. I believe I worked through some things at this point, simply because I realized that in those tough times, I was going to have to get tough. There were no other options.

Grandma had helped me through a difficult spot, but that door was now closed. The idea of someone cuddling and comforting me was not an option. As a result, this was one of the most difficult, challenging times of my life, and also one of the most beneficial.

Life Lesson #11: Don't sweat the small stuff, it can evolve into mental avalanches.

As I BEGAN to make changes in my life, I decided to play football for our small high school. It seemed like the prettiest girls always liked the football guys. Besides, I liked contact sports, so I knew it would be fun. I played as a defensive tackle. The only problem was that I had never played before.

At one point, I finally confessed to Coach Williams that I didn't understand the plays.

He said, "I know you don't, Henderson, but you've got a lot of heart, so here's the deal: when the ball moves, all you need to do is just get the quarterback."

I didn't know much about the science of the game, but I understood that simple concept. I evolved into a respectable player, starting in every game.

Playing football meant I associated less with the rough crowd and didn't drink as much. I felt good about my new identity, and in a way, playing football helped me cope with my feelings of need and inferiority.

But even with all of that effort, in my heart I still felt like a piece of the puzzle was missing. I kept wondering what else was out there that could help fill the emptiness. I felt there had to be something more to life. I just didn't know what it was.

Life Lesson #12: If your heart is in whatever you are doing, your shortcomings can be worked out.

IV

THE TIDE BEGINS
TO TURN

IT WAS a typical Friday afternoon in crafts class, and I had a low level of motivation for studying. Instead, I was more interested in getting hyped up for a home game followed by a night of raising hell and drinking beer. As a bunch of us football players sat around the table, a cute little cheerleader asked us if we wanted to go to church with her on Sunday night. Lois had curly dark hair, beautiful eyes, and a radiant smile.

In the past, the nice girls made it a habit to stay away from the likes of me. They decided that I wasn't their type, what with all the high-risk activities, a police record, and an overindulgence in alcohol. When Lois showed an interest, even though it was just friendly, it got my attention. All I wanted to do was get closer to her. And if going to church would allow me to get my foot in the door and my body in her bed, then I was ready for some old-time religion.

At the time, I felt that church was a place for sissies. While living with Grandma as a kid, she had required me to go to church with the girls while my brother and uncle got to stay home and wrestle and watch Roy Rogers and Gene Autry. It didn't do much to make me feel like going to church was worth the effort.

Another prejudice I had about church came from the pastor's sermons I'd heard. God was angry about my sins, and after I died, there was going to be a big price to pay. I thought God was mean and mad and looking to kick somebody's ass on any given day.

I understood the gravity of my own shortcomings, and it didn't seem necessary to be reminded of them on a weekly basis.

However, if Lois was going to be at church with her perfectly shaped figure, I thought it would be a good idea if I were there too. I was in, no matter what she wanted to do. She could have invited us to clean bathrooms at road side parks, and I would have had my johnny mop in hand, ready to do business. I was just honored to be included.

My experience at church that night proved to be much different from what I had expected. The preacher talked about basic conflicts that a lot of young people encounter. The message was titled, *A Battle With the 3 P's*. The minister said some of us had encountered conflicts with our parents, some with the principals at our schools, and still others had been in trouble with the police. I thought he must have been reading my diary. He went on to say that these conflicts would exist until we made peace with God through Christ.

Something about the message drew my attention. Up until then, my life had been empty and filled with loneliness. As I thought about the pastor's words, I reflected back to all of the substances I had sniffed and drunk, just trying to skew reality and make life more bearable. It seemed like everything I tried had quit working. Some would describe it as the calling of the Holy Spirit. In AA, we call it a moment of clarity.

In the quietness of my heart, I thought, *Try it, Ron. Why not? Nothing else has worked. This might be the answer.*

Then I had another thought: *This dude probably has a Master's Degree in "Trickinology."* I suddenly became convinced he was trying to trick me through some form of religious hypnotism, and I needed to get out of there before the virus spread. I immediately left the church. I figured my interest in what he was saying would soon pass, like a bad case of diarrhea. When the spell left me, I would be able to get back to my normal life as I had always known it.

However, what the preacher had said that evening couldn't be dismissed. The words kept coming back to me. I was forced to admit that my life was lacking something I desperately needed. I was ingesting alcohol to fill the vacancy, but it wasn't working. Yes, my consumption of alcohol had already been radically reduced. Yes, I was hanging with a more respectable group of guys on my football team. But my life was still like a house that was all clean and swept, yet empty, without furniture.

I can still recall the vivid words that kept ringing in my head, long after I left the church service: *Why not try it, Ron? You've been drunk, high, locked up, beat up, knocked out, and kicked out. You have nothing to lose, and nothing else has worked.*

Soon, I went back to that little country church in Wayside, Kansas. This time I went alone, without the influence of a cute cheerleader or any of my buddies. Honestly, I didn't even hear what subject the pastor addressed, because I wasn't there to listen to his message. I was there to do something about what he'd said the first time I visited. At the end of the service, the pastor said if anybody wanted to yield their life to Jesus Christ, they should step forward now. It was just that simple.

Maybe the shortest prayer ever uttered from a human mouth was uttered by me as I walked down the aisle to the front of the room: *God, I have made a mess of my life. If you can do anything with it, I give it to you.*

As soon as I gave my heart to God, I felt a sudden shift. It wasn't like I saw a bright light or anything. But a calmness and peace pervaded my heart. I felt a tremendous relief, as if a fifty-pound weight had been lifted from my back, a weight I had been carrying all of my life. I understood the word *peace* for the first time. The feeling remained with me, a high like I'd never experienced before.

Though nothing ever developed between me and Lois, her brave, kind invitation to church proved to be the glue that has held me together for the past forty-plus years. I'm forever grateful for that.

Life Lesson #13: Sometimes God speaks to you through unexpected means, like girls with beautiful eyes and dark curly hair. At those times, it's important to listen.

AFTER THAT EXPERIENCE, my life took a different turn. It seemed impossible to restrain myself from sharing my excitement about my new lease on life. I'd stand on the hood of my '67 Plymouth Belvedere at Mohawk Park in Tulsa, crying out on a bullhorn to bikers and hippies about my newfound faith. I was naïve enough to believe that as soon as they heard the good news, they'd all run up to the bumper of my car and beg to hear more, but that never happened. Instead, they just turned up their music and told me to shut the heck up!

My passion for preaching about God centered on my desire to connect with any young man who was as troubled as I had been and tell him how my life had changed. I understood what it was like to be a kid consumed with fear and insecurity, uncertain about the meaning of life, and I wanted to share with someone like me how the grace of God had touched my lonely, empty life. I wanted to make a difference.

I was zealous about my faith. It seemed I had found the pearl of great price to which Jesus compared the kingdom of God in Matthew 13:45–46. I naively believed that if I simply explained how the experience had radically altered my life, others would also want a taste of this new wine that had touched my lips.

In our tiny town in southeast Kansas, there wasn't much for young people to do besides drink beer and fight. At the ripe age of twenty, I started a recreation center for teenagers known as the Sunshine Youth Center. Civic organizations got involved with this effort, helping raise funds to support it. We held events such as pancake breakfasts and boxing tournaments. In the small community of 2,500 people, I was voted Man of the Year for my accomplishments. It was amazing to feel successful for helping others, without the support of alcohol to fuel me.

The rec center was a fun place for kids to come and hang out. There was a lot for them to do, like shoot pool and play foosball, air hockey, and ping pong. When the facility was full of teenagers, I'd stand on the counter with my Bible in one hand, sharing about my newfound faith. I saw myself as a type of John the Baptist. Looking back today, I realize they probably saw me as a Jesus freak on dope. However, the kids also sensed that I was genuinely concerned about them, so they accepted my unconventional style.

I also enrolled in a community college, preparing for a major in psychology. I had a living space in the attic of the rec center, and through the money earned from the pool tables, foosball, and air hockey, I was able to make enough to survive. A dear instructor at the college encouraged me to consider attending a small private bible college in Kansas City. She stated that in her opinion, God could use me in full-time ministry.

Although Mrs. Zoscke was the mother of fourteen children, she was still willing to help pay my tuition. I was deeply moved by her kindness and generosity. However, I had some reservations about being in the ministry. My experiences with the clergy was skewed. It seemed like most of the clergy I ever talked to spoke in a sheepish voice; they were quiet and demure, and they shook hands like a dead fish.

By comparison, I was raised around drinking, fighting, and a lot of yelling. I'd lived a hard life already. My background was different than that of many Christians I had met, and I was afraid I wouldn't fit in.

However, within two years, something changed in me. I found myself on the way to Calvary Bible College in Kansas City. With enough encouragement from Mrs. Zoscke and others in our community, I finally decided it would be for the greater good if I pursued the ministry.

When I arrived on campus, the president of the college informed me that I would be placed on academic probation and I would have to get a haircut. If I didn't like his mandate, I could just take my five-hundred-dollar camper back to wherever I came from. Submitting to authority has never been one of my strongest traits. Nevertheless, I sold my trailer, got a haircut, and moved into the dormitories.

While attending Calvary Bible College, I regularly stood in front of the bus stop and passed out Gospel tracts, telling everyone how a fall-down drunk with suicidal ideations had been dramatically changed by God. I was sure they wanted to know, because they always just sat there in rapt attention and listened. Sometime later, it occurred to me they were just waiting for their bus to arrive and were probably glad when it finally did.

After graduation, I soon married a wonderful woman. Ann loved God, and she was very beautiful. In most ways, Ann was the complete opposite of me. She came from a conservative Christian home. She had never drunk or smoked anything.

I was drawn to her and her family because their life seemed so stable and calm, whereas my life had been like an ongoing train wreck. Her father had been a pastor. When we met, she was employed at a Christian radio station, and I was attracted to her strong work ethic. She worked a lot of hours and loved what she did. I loved her for all those reasons and more.

We served in Kansas City at a very conservative church. Looking back at my tenure, I have come to the conclusion that many well-meaning people—Christian leaders—add a lot to their doctrine that isn't biblical. Some will mask themselves under the umbrella of God, but the message of love and grace gets lost.

However, if this false dogma is preached long enough, people accept it as truth. In those days, the hot topics that were common in sermons included: *God said our sideburns shouldn't pass beyond our earlobes. Our mustaches must not extend beyond the corner of our lips. No hair on a man's head should ever touch his collar. If the music we listened to didn't have a piano and harp, it was probably of the devil. And women are not allowed to wear slacks or jeans.*

The death blow to our time at that church was when the senior pastor told me I needed to reach twenty families for Jesus, persuade them to give ten percent of their income to the church, and if I was successful, I could retain my job.

We left Kansas City for a church in a suburb of Chicago:

LaGrange Bible Church. Pastor Hovey was one of the most caring gentlemen I'd ever known. He was short in stature, tall in kindness, and missing most of his hair. We had a rewarding time working with college age kids and young couples. We ate at great restaurants, had a meaningful ministry, and enjoyed a well-balanced home and work life. Ann got pregnant with our first child during our tenure at La Grange. It was one of the most rewarding times of my life.

At this point, it had been almost ten years since I had last felt the need to drink. It wasn't that I vowed to never consume alcohol; I just didn't feel the need. It was like God had filled my life with a sense of wholeness and purpose, and there was no void left to fill.

Life Lesson #14: Overindulgence isn't essential, especially if you have made peace with God.

AFTER A FEW YEARS AT LaGRANGE, we set off for the seminary in Dallas to study the scriptures in the original Greek language. Ann gave birth to a wonderful, sensitive baby girl—Megan—and a mischievous little boy—Tyler. In order to get Megan to take a nap, sometimes I'd put her in the back seat of my '57 Chevy with very loud pipes, much to Ann's utter frustration. Just a few miles down the road, and Megan would be sound asleep every time. Tyler was a sweet, gentle, rough-and-tumble daddy's boy. Megan would make mud pies and want to put them in the microwave. All Tyler wanted to do was throw the mud at his sister.

For a while, life seemed perfect. Unfortunately, that time of happiness didn't last. It was while we were living in Dallas when my interest in drinking was born again. And it's something I came to regret.

There are several reasons I resumed my drinking habits after going twelve years without touching a drop to my lips. For one thing, I had become more arrogant and self-centered in my Christian walk. Pride crept its way into my life. And why shouldn't I be proud? After all, I was attending one of the finest theological institutions in the country—Dallas Theological Seminary. At least I thought it was one of the finest. And I thought I was one of the finest students there.

Initially, when I set out on this spiritual journey, I was simply on a quest to find a young man who had suffered some of the same struggles in life that I had and offer him hope. In those days, I was like a beggar with a piece of bread looking for another hungry man to share it with. If I found him, my mission would be accomplished. If I was fortunate, I'd find another person to share with too.

But eventually, my studies became merely academic and intellectual, and I didn't feel the same sense of gratitude and humility that I had embraced earlier in my Christian experience. Somewhere between studying the book of Genesis and the book of Revelation, I lost my way.

Life Lesson #15: As your knowledge and feelings of importance increase, sometimes your self-absorption and pride increase at a faster rate.

In the Big Book, the text used in Alcoholics Anonymous, it says that alcohol is "cunning, baffling, and powerful." I understand that concept firsthand. As I went through my time in Dallas, I gradually shifted from a spiritual emphasis to an academic emphasis. As a result, the Bible became just another textbook. It was something to be analyzed, but it was no longer alive or life-changing to me. I stopped living it as zealously as I once had.

As our knowledge increases, sometimes our sense of pride does also. That's not to say that everyone who has earned graduate-level training is egotistical and arrogant; it just happened that way for me. Because of the spiritual pride I gained at the seminary, I began to wander away from the God I had loved. Instead of being God-focused, I became more self-absorbed, puffed up with the knowledge I was obtaining.

Pride has a subtle way of creeping into our lives and taking over. But it isn't satisfying. It doesn't fill our needs. as I grew more prideful, I grew less connected to my true purpose in life. When the peace that my Lord had freely given me was absent, I felt empty and void of meaning in my life yet again. So, I created my own form of fulfillment with alcohol.

For a real alcoholic, when we defect from our Higher Power, a relapse is imminent. And that's what happened to me. By all outward appearances, I still looked just like the rest of my classmates—neatly cropped hair, blue blazer and khaki pants. Jesus described guys like me in Matthew 15:7–8 (*New Living Translation*): "You hypocrites! Isaiah was right when he prophesied about you, for he wrote, 'These people honor me with their lips, but their hearts are far from me.'"

I'll say this again: Not everybody who becomes a student of the scriptures gets drunk, jeopardizes his life and the safety of others, gets fired, and loses a home. It was just the route I took. But I want my life to be an example to others of what not to do, as well as how God's grace is greater even than our biggest mistakes.

Ann began to notice my problem with alcohol. Because she

didn't know any of the details of my drinking habits as a teenager, she didn't know how close I was to a relapse. She would say, "Ron, I think you're drinking too much."

My response was always the same: "I've just had one drink!"

The only problem was, that one drink started with an 8-ounce portion of alcohol, then progressed to a 12-, 16-, 32-, and finally a 46-ounce drink. So, we were technically both right. In those days, I did just have one drink—the size of my one drink just got bigger and more potent.

Three years later, I stumbled across the stage and accepted a Master's Degree in Biblical Studies. I was working for an educational and political organization known as Dallas Right to Life at the time, and my primary responsibilities entailed giving presentations in high schools and colleges, as well as raising funds. The only important rule the director laid down was, "Do not consume alcohol at political events!" But I regularly defied that rule. Pride and defiance were creeping their way more and more into my life.

One night during a political event, I consumed numerous glasses of wine, against the wishes of my supervisor. As the server came to our table to offer drinks, I'd chug my glass and order another before she could even get a few steps away. How many drinks did I have? I don't know, but I'd had enough to roll my Nissan 300ZX with the T-tops off. Of course, I wasn't wearing a seat belt. The car rolled three times on Hawn Freeway.

Miraculously, all I suffered as a result of the accident were a few bruises and a mouth full of dirt. For a long time, I tried to make myself and others believe the accident occurred because of a blown tire. The reality? I didn't have a blown tire. It was the alcohol.

I don't think anybody else ever believed me, but by golly, I wanted to believe me. In order to get and stay sober, it says in the Big Book, "we must be rigorously honest." At this time in my life, I lacked honesty. I wasn't willing to admit that I had a problem.

After all, I was a Christian. I was a Bible College and Seminary graduate. How could I have a drinking problem?

Before the dust settled from the wreck, a kind highway patrolman was at the scene of the accident inquiring if I needed to go to the hospital. I told him I was okay. If he would graciously take me home, I would be deeply indebted, I only lived a few miles from the accident. Instead of taking me to the hospital or home, he then offered to take me to jail.

I said, "That's mighty nice of you to offer, Mr. Highway Patrolman, but I would just as soon go home."

He said, "I insist."

"Okay, have it your way, Mr. Highway Patrolman."

The officer also insisted that I sit in the back seat with handcuffs on. My house was a lot closer than the Dallas County Jail, but I didn't think pointing this out would make any difference.

The next day, an article in the paper was titled, "Pro Life Leader Arrested for DUI." That was the beginning of the end. I lost my job, our house was foreclosed on, and we were broke.

Life Lesson #16: The life for most drunks is a long, rough road—most of it is unpaved and uneven.

ANN'S PARENTS lived in Omaha, and they invited us to move there. As you might imagine, I didn't have too many churches seriously looking to hire me. To be honest, I didn't have any—so off for Omaha we headed.

Warren and Gladys were incredibly kind, and they helped us get back on our feet financially. Our second son, Evan, was born in Omaha; he busted out of his mother's womb ready to take on the world. We have always teased him that he was a legend in his own mind. He's grown into a handsome young man, full of confidence and charisma. He's just flat out fun to be around.

My first job in Omaha was as a sales rep/trainer for an industrial laboratory. It wasn't as impressive as it sounds. Our top-selling product was a toilet bowel cleaner, guaranteed to remove calcium and "other kinds" of deposits. Yuck.

Every other week, I stayed in Omaha and worked my territory. The other weeks, I traveled throughout the Midwest, training new sales reps. Because of this, the job proved to be perfect for a person with a strong predilection for alcohol. It provided a superb opportunity to drink as much as I wanted during the weeks that I was traveling. Most of the time, I was even able to work the next day.

However, at our annual sales meeting in Chicago, my behavior slipped below acceptable levels. At one point, the district sales manager had to call my room to wake me for a meeting I was supposed to be attending. I had gotten really drunk the night before and had come down with a bad case of "anal glaucoma."

To translate for the non-alcoholics, that term means I just couldn't see my drunken ass getting out of bed. My drinking habit was beginning to bother me somewhat, but I tried not to dwell on it too much. In the world of psychology, it's called denial.

Fortunately, I didn't lose my job. But my love for alcohol seemed to be increasing. It was like an animal that occasionally slipped out of its cage. As long as the beast stayed contained, life was relatively peaceful.

Ann was not aware of my episodes of drunkenness at this

point. It was one of those subjects I chose not to share with too many people. Maybe it was out of shame, or maybe I simply wasn't ready to admit I had a problem. I didn't want anybody confusing me with the facts, so I kept my habit a secret. During this stage of drinking, I was like a stealth bomber—able to fly under the radar.

As I fought the moral dilemma that my drinking problem posed, I also felt a calling from God. I loved the preparation and delivery of the scriptures to a crowd, and I missed it.

I felt like I should have been investing my time in the lives of others, guiding them to the light that had brightened my life at one point. In a way, I felt like a sick guy at the hospital on a quest to heal others—I wanted to touch others in a positive way, without passing on the virus I was carrying.

My father-in-law was president of a Bible college in Omaha, and he was always aware of opportunities for involvement. Warren told me about a little church located just across the river in Council Bluffs, Iowa. The congregation wanted a guest speaker for their Sunday night service, and I enthusiastically accepted the invitation, since my itinerary for speaking engagements was pretty empty.

Life Lesson #17: Focus on healing yourself first; people who are sick are unable to help others.

WHEN I ARRIVED at the church, I realized that I definitely wouldn't be speaking at the Crystal Cathedral. The congregation met only on Sunday nights because the building belonged to another church that conducted services in the mornings. After I spoke, a silver-haired woman approached me. She looked as if she would normally have a strong sense self-confidence, but at the moment, she looked timid. She confided that this would be their last night to meet together. They had tried for years to get their church established in the community, but they had reached a point where the discouraged little flock was ready to pull the plug on the whole operation.

They told me that they would continue to meet if I was willing to be their pastor. I was stunned—the congregation hardly knew me. It was like asking a girl to marry you on the first date. They were a small group, but let's face it: I wasn't the hottest show in town either. I had graduated from the seminary about a year and a half earlier, and since that time, I'd managed to start drinking again, total a car, get fired, lose my house, and create a lot of pain for others. I should have felt honored that they would allow me to attend their church, much less be their pastor. After a few minutes of thought and prayer, I agreed to do it.

During my next two years as the pastor of Midlands Evangelical Free Church in Council Bluffs, I stayed sober. Life was pleasant and stable. My relationship with God was meaningful again, and I was finding fulfillment in serving others. The congregation began to grow; we bought twenty-eight acres of rural land to build a comfortable little country church.

However, I didn't feel that I could truly identify with stable, conservative farmers as much I could with misfits and mavericks. The population I felt called to was that of recovering drunks and junkies, flavored with a few convicted felons, not retired farmers and rednecks.

I wanted to trade our land for a formerly wild, infamous rock and roll bar. My gut feeling was that we needed to attract some of the former constituents from the bar to our church. Eventually, the owner of the bar agreed to trade our property for his. I thought the old bar's reputation would be perfect in helping us reach our target population.

Half of the congregation saw the benefit of this approach; the other half was vehemently opposed to the idea. Rather than try to change the minds of our older members or orchestrate a church split, Ann and I decided to take our unconventional philosophy on down the road. Council Bluffs preferred organs and pianos, but I dreamed of a church with drums and guitars, long hair, and cutoff jeans.

I was in search of a community that was more like-minded. My search led me to a pastor's conference in Chicago. As I networked among the various leaders, I was introduced to a gentleman by the name of Rick Penner. Rick was from the southwest region of New Mexico and Arizona.

When I shared my vision with Rick, he encouraged me to come to Phoenix. He said, "Rather than looking for an unorthodox church such as you have described, just start one. Otherwise, you probably won't find it."

That was all I needed to hear. I knew a little bit about starting an organization. After all, I started a youth center while in college, as well as a successful window washing business in while I was in the seminary. Starting a church couldn't be much different. I rushed home and told Ann, and she reluctantly bought into the plan. We loaded our "congregation"—our kids—into the front seat of a U-Haul truck and headed for Phoenix.

I liked everything about Phoenix: the sun, the bright-colored shirts, the palm trees, and the laid-back, casual attitude toward life. This was my kind of place. Our church, which we named Deer Canyon Community Church, was slow getting started, but within two years, growth was happening. Our congregation was blessed with some gifted musicians, complete with long hair and cutoffs. This was in the early 90s, when the American church was transitioning from traditional to a more contemporary style of worship. And our church fit right in. During this time, our fourth child, Veronica was born. What a beautiful, innocent little human being! It seemed like from an early age she had the mind and ability to speak on the level of an adult. She would absorb herself in books when most little girls were playing with dolls, and she asked so many questions that her brothers wanted to pull her long blond hair out and choke her with it.

At first, my time in Phoenix was productive. I was highly motivated and loved what I was doing. The congregation and I meshed well. They were made up of formerly unchurched people, mostly in their mid-thirties to early-forties. People were being reached, and the church was growing. In many ways, it was a perfect situation.

Ann and I lived with our children in a spacious house on a few acres at the edge of town. The large garage we had on the back part of the property was an ideal place to restore the '55 Chevrolet Nomad that I had dragged with us from Iowa. It was a perfect project: the car required a total restoration, and I loved everything about the process of working on an old car. After a day spent taking care of the usual matters pertaining to church, I spent evenings in the shop. It proved to be relaxing and therapeutic.

The only element missing was a cold bottle of beer to take the edge off of a long day. At least, that was my rationale. I believed that Ann wouldn't be all that supportive of my individual counseling session with a bottle of beer, so I never bothered to tell her. I'd drink beer and work until she went to sleep.

In a few months, the pendulum had subtly shifted once again. Drinking beer became my primary purpose, and occasionally I'd work on the Nomad. This approach had such a relaxing, sedative effect. I wondered if it would have the same relaxing effect when I stood behind the podium on Sunday morning. A subtle sense of my old neediness began to creep back in.

The whole situation was ironic. I was being invited to speak at conferences. We were seeing growth in our church. And we had a beautiful home. I was a success! But as I've said earlier, pride is an elusive enemy—it subtly slipped in and began to pervade my thinking.

At the same time, I was beginning to make a departure from God in my spiritual life. Before long, I was like that same empty vessel I had been as a teenager before I became a Christian. It would have helped me tremendously if I'd been willing to reach out to other pastors for help, but I didn't want to admit that I was struggling and sinking.

Well-intentioned Christians have asked me at times, "Ron, how could you be so selfish?" This question implies that all a person has to do to solve their addiction is decide not to be selfish. If only it were that easy.

The simplest way to describe my behavior would be to imagine myself as a deer hunter shooting blanks with his rifle: I looked like I knew what I was doing and made a lot of noise. But I wasn't the same person on the inside that I projected on the outside. Outwardly, I projected confidence. Inwardly, I was anything but that. I wanted to cover up my fear and shame, and alcohol was an adequate assistant.

I knew my effectiveness was limited when I was drinking. But I also believed that if I could act enthusiastic enough and use bullets that made a loud boom, the rest of the deer would never know the difference. They'd think the hunter had arrived. Like a lot of people struggling with an addiction, I became skilled at lying to myself.

As a result of all this, I drifted away from the God I had learned to love, and subtly started a perverted form of self-worship. My drink of choice was vodka. I had been told the odor wasn't as noticeable as beer or whiskey. It became standard procedure to chug a half-pint of 80-proof vodka before I preached. When the brethren thought I was in my study praying, I was actually pouring myself a strong one. I was beginning to live a dual life, and my addiction to alcohol was increasing.

It was a major error, but I wasn't willing to admit that I had a problem to myself or anyone else. And as long as nobody else noticed the truth, the only one I had to convince was me. It's been said that we are only as sick as our deepest secrets. I knew that I could never admit that I had a problem because if I did, I would have to find a solution.

Life Lesson #18: *As the saying goes: we are only as sick as our deepest secrets.*

To all outward appearances, my charade seemed to be working—for the moment. But sadly, the spiritual condition of my heart didn't beat for God or the pastorate.

Alcohol resumed its place on the throne of my life, once again becoming my master. If it controls your time, money, much of your thoughts, and who your friends are...that pretty much fits the criteria of a master.

When you worship this god, he becomes more and more demanding. In the initial stages, it starts out as a party—fun and games. For a time, it can give you a warm, fuzzy, tingly, euphoric feeling, a real sense of identity. But then the life of addiction becomes slavery and bondage.

A close friend of mine was recently reminiscing about the past, and he said, "I reached a point in my drinking that I knew I had a problem. I just didn't think there was any way to escape my addiction, and it would probably take me to the grave."

I laughed and said, "The difference between you and me is like two guys who have egg on their face. The first guy believes he has egg on his face but thinks it is stuck there until he dies. Then there is the second guy, who refuses to look into the mirror and tries to make himself believe there is nothing wrong. 'That's not egg on my face; it's just dry skin,' he tells himself."

Unfortunately, I was like the second guy: living a secret lie that I wouldn't even admit to myself. As I look back now, I can see how that self-deception and refusal to bring my problem into the light of day meant that I was heading down a slow, grey road to hell and destruction.

Life Lesson #19: In the end, the life of the addict becomes that of slavery and bondage. If he doesn't change, he is destined to travel a slow, grey road of pain and misery.

My DRUG and alcohol counselor once compared alcoholism to the trimesters of a pregnancy. The addiction starts without many noticeable, outward changes. By the last trimester, however, the changes are obvious. But instead of bringing forth life, the addiction takes you toward death.

The counselor also said that my drinking habits prior to committing to getting help were probably the equivalent to being at the end of the second trimester. I was experiencing a fair amount of pain and discomfort. A little bit of kicking. Running out of room. If you add the symptoms of getting fired, losing my house, and being dead broke, then I was definitely in the second trimester during my time in Phoenix.

How far is an addict willing to go before they feel the desire to truly change? It really depends upon how far down we choose to ride the elevator, so to speak.

A lot of folks in the first stages have said, "Well, I've caused enough pain and misery to myself and others... It's been a fun ride, but I think I'll get off on this floor." They are the smart ones. I've had other friends who took the elevator all the way down to the basement, and then went six feet deeper than that.

It's easy to be critical of addicts if you have never struggled with addiction yourself. Many people ask, "Why don't you just quit?" My only answer is that when our addiction's demonic tentacles begin to wrap around our neck, the control it has over us is simply unimaginable and irresistible.

Life Lesson #20: Though addiction is life-threatening, it is not easy to break its chokehold over us. It's a terrible master.

THESE LESSONS I've just described are things I learned later in life, when I finally hit my rock bottom. But while I was pastoring in Phoenix, I hadn't yet reached that point of desperation. Sadly, I made some terrible decisions during that time in my life.

At one point during those years in Phoenix, I was invited to speak at a Bible conference in Tucson. I jumped at the opportunity, for all the wrong reasons. I knew it would be the perfect place to feed my massive ego, and a great chance to drink. So, I did the two things I loved most.

First, I talked to the crowd with fervor and enthusiasm. After the event, I went back to my room to carefully examine my delivery. *How did I do? Was I funny but not too funny? Did I look sharp in my dark blue suit? Will they invite me back? Is my popularity growing? Am I building a reputation as a gifted speaker?*

After my careful analysis was complete, I headed off to find a bar. I prowled the streets of Tucson in search of respectable looking establishment that was worthy of a man of my stature. Before long, I drove past a bar with fifteen or so Harleys out front. *This must be the place!* With my business suit and neatly cropped hair, I made a concerted effort to switch my persona from prolific preacher to badass biker.

At first, I felt a little awkward. But after a few hours of drinking whiskey and Coke, I seemed to forget who I was. Around two in the morning, the rough-looking bar maid still looked rough. She announced to the patrons that it was last call for alcohol. Just to make sure I had enough courage in me to face my departure, I ordered two doubles, chugged them down and stumbled out to my bike.

Living a double life isn't easy, but with the assistance of our good friend Jack Daniels, I was able to play the role well. Eventually, though, as you might guess, that way of life caught up with me.

Life Lesson #21: Living a double life isn't easy, and alcohol only helps you play the roles for a while.

ANOTHER PASTOR'S conference was scheduled in Newark, New Jersey, a few months later. This would be another outlet to feed the monster of alcohol that was raging inside, all in the name of being a devoted pastor. At the conference, my acting skills were in full blossom. I attended the meetings where I thought my presence was needed, and afterwards I headed for a bar.

As I made an effort to take an honest look back at my motives during this time, it had little to do with wanting to go to a conference, gain more knowledge and be of greater service to my congregation. I had been told that if I showed up for the gathering, there might be a chance that I could speak before the crowd and tell everybody how great I was and how my church was growing so rapidly. It's hard to tell which was greater—my addiction to alcohol or my addiction to self. I was so focused on me and my career that my inner life felt unsatisfying, fueling the compelling need to medicate my mind with alcohol.

When I was informed that I wasn't going to get to speak at the conference in New Jersey, my pride took a hard blow. As I faced the grim reality that this would not be the time for my fifteen minutes of fame, I left the conference early and proceeded to drink heavily for a few hours, trying to ease my hurt pride.

Around ten o'clock that evening, I jumped on my bike and headed back to Phoenix. Whenever I stopped for gas, I also stopped to drink beer. That night, I rode from Newark to Chicago, non-stop—approximately a thousand miles. I did it while drunk and tired, but I made it.

The love of God has been demonstrated to me time and time again, gently nudging me, saying, "I love you even when you are not very lovable. I will protect you even if you are not aware of my presence." This was a perfect example of how He loves us. I finished the final leg from Chicago to Phoenix without any accidents. His intervening grace abounds, even when we're not offering anything in return.

Life Lesson #22: God's intervening grace abounds toward us in spite of our failures and flaws.

In August 1992, I planned a long getaway on my bike. Out of courtesy, I invited Ann, knowing she wouldn't want to ride with me. She claimed I rode too fast and was too reckless; she had fears that someday I would be in a fatal accident. And besides, somebody had to stay home to be with the kids.

I told her that I wanted to go to Denver in search of a brother who was reportedly given up by my parents for adoption at an early age. In truth, I had minimal interest in the research project, and much more of an interest in feeding my addiction. If I went on a binge out of town, no one would know, and I could maintain my respected position as a pastor at home.

Once again, the distorted thinking that happened when I was drinking kicked in. I convinced myself that a few beers on my way out of town wouldn't hurt. On the contrary—it would make the drive more pleasant. I recall hiding behind a QuikTrip, chugging the beer down like a man who had been on a deserted island without fresh water for days.

By the time I reached Holbrook, Arizona, about 150 miles from Phoenix, I was falling down drunk. But not too drunk that I couldn't stumble into a bar and have a few more. By the time the bar closed, I couldn't walk in a straight line, much less ride in a straight line, but I decided to head for Denver anyway. Of course, the entire plan made perfectly good sense at the time.

What happened after that has been reported to me, but I actually remember very little of it all. The accident occurred about five miles east of Holbrook, when I passed out while driving. I'm not sure how fast I was going, but the speed limit was 75 miles per hour. Motorists had reported to the police that I was weaving back and forth as I passed them on Interstate 40.

A truck driver explained to the emergency first responders that she had swerved around a large object lying in the road, thinking it must have been a dead deer. A few hundred feet down the interstate, she spotted my motorcycle lying down in the middle of the road and realized most deer don't ride Electra Glide Classics. The hospital in Holbrook wasn't equipped to handle my injuries, so they life-flighted me back to Flagstaff, about a hundred miles west.

The medical report indicated that I had suffered numerous broken bones: ribs, hand, collarbone and face. Worst of all, I experienced a subdural hematoma—a form of traumatic brain injury in which blood gathers between the dura (the outer protective covering of the brain) and the arachnoid (the middle layer of the meninges).

Subdural hemorrhages can cause an increase in intracranial pressure, which can cause compression of and damage to delicate brain tissue, resulting in brain damage. That is, if you survive—the mortality rate for this injury is around sixty to eighty percent. Fortunately, my skull was cracked in the accident, so as my brain started to swell, the pressure was able to expand without causing permanent brain damage or death.

I regained consciousness in the hospital in Flagstaff, with bandages covering my body from head to toe. The family was notified of the accident and had immediately come to the hospital.

Tyler, my oldest son, was the first to enter the room. As soon as he saw me, he turned to the nurse and said, "Dad's not in this room. They gave us the wrong room number." The nurse told him that I was indeed his father.

Ann dropped her head and began to sob. With my swollen head, and all my bandages and broken bones, I looked like a freak at a carnival show.

I was homebound for several months, while healing from all my injuries. Climbing out of bed was an arduous task, so I just lay there most of the time. The congregation never knew the exact nature of the accident. I recall explaining to them that it was all related to stress and fatigue, as if I held them responsible for my problems.

I still wasn't willing to admit that I had a serious drinking problem. Ann was hurt and angry with me, but I reassured her that the accident wasn't related to my drinking. I claimed it was simply that the pressures of ministry had weighed heavy on my shoulders. Of course, anyone with an IQ of six wouldn't have believed such a preposterous story, and she didn't either.

Eventually I was able to resume my position as pastor. The congregation still didn't know I was living a lie. For the next year, my drinking was hidden but it did continue. The god of alcohol that wanted to destroy me had replaced the true God who loved me. If my god of alcohol demanded that I consume it in order to be whole, I obeyed my master. Temporarily, it seemed to work. My addiction made me feel complete, but I still didn't realize I was on a slippery slope that would lead to further misery and pain to myself and others.

My predicament back then reminds me now of a situation I'd gotten myself into when I used to fly a small Cessna 172 plane. One afternoon I left Wichita, bound for Kansas City. I thought I could fly without setting the instruments to guide me. Initially, I figured I was just slightly off course. But a few hours later as darkness set in, I realized I was out of fuel and had no idea where I was. Additionally, I had never flown at night without the assistance of my instructor.

I radioed to the nearest control tower and was informed that I was about 25 miles north of Joplin, Missouri. I was petrified that I was going to crash and burn in a farmer's field and not be found for years. Fortunately, with the patience of the man in the air traffic control tower, I found my way, landed, and climbed out of the plane, jumping up and down with joy that I was still alive. After refueling and setting my instruments, I got back on course and finally reached my destination.

I think sometimes it's valuable to lose your way and be low on fuel, provided you are willing to cry out to the tower and admit you are lost. As I write this, I feel a sense of regret that I waited so long to call out for help, that I had been so unwilling to admit that I had lost my way. I never set out to be a pastor who chugged vodka before I preached. It was a slow, subtle decision that eventually took control over my life. It was similar to flying at night in a strange land. At first I was only slightly off course, but the farther I went, the more I was off course, low on fuel, filled with fear, and having no idea where I was.

Life Lesson #23: Sometimes it's good to lose your way if the result is that you call out to the control tower in desperation, asking for help.

THE EXCUSE for my next drinking binge was a pastor's conference in Minneapolis, Minnesota. The timing was perfect. It was being held during the same time as the renowned bike rally in Sturgis, South Dakota.

Shortly after I left Phoenix on my bike, the drinking started all over again. I stopped for the night in a little town in New Mexico, and after closing the bar down, I drifted off to sleep on a table at a nearby campground. The next day, I continued my journey, having an occasional drink when I stopped for gas. By the time I got to Denver, I felt that I deserved a longer break. I found a cozy little bar/restaurant, and the worship service resumed where it left off the night before.

Without trying to make excuses for my behavior, I can only speak to what was happening in my heart and mind. It was that old self-obsession with misery that started up my drinking again. Alcohol covered up the misery in a temporary way, and it helped numb my empty heart.

For those who have never suffered from alcohol dependency, the concept probably seems foreign. Christian friends have said to me, "You were just a selfish, inconsiderate, carnal, self-indulgent bum." I would tend to agree, but the bondage of alcoholism extends beyond such a simplistic response. Alcoholism reaches the very core of a man's values. It tells him how to spend his leisure time. It controls his money, mind, body, and soul.

After staying at the bar in Denver for several hours, I got back on my bike and headed north. The sun began to set as I rolled into Cheyenne, Wyoming. Immediately I began looking for a room and a bar, preferably close together. My perception of Cheyenne was that it was like a Wild West town, full of action and excitement. Riding motorcycles often gives one the feeling of freedom and adventure, similar to what cowboys in the Wild West must have felt. My version just happened to be on a black iron horse instead of a real one.

Freedom and adventure are two common components missing

from our lives as we move into adulthood and maturity. Our passion for risk and challenges is replaced with concern for a 401(k) and security. I believe that is part of the reason I found this risky behavior so tempting. Riding my bike offered a release from my middle-aged fear of fading away into the sunset of dull complacency and boredom.

Life Lesson #24: Freedom and adventure are missing today, many have traded them for security, safety, and acceptance.

AND I STILL THINK A LITTLE adventure is healthy, if handled properly. The mistake I made was mixing in alcohol with my riding. It was a combustible combination—and now it was about to explode on me.

Little did I know that as I stepped into that tiny, dimly-lit Cheyenne tavern, hearing Hank Williams blaring on the jukebox, it would be the last time I would ever stand behind the pulpit proclaiming God's word. The atmosphere in the bar was most bizarre—it was a stark contrast between stereotypical redneck hillbillies with wrinkled hats and cowboy boots, and hardcore bikers covered with chains and tattoos.

I nestled into a corner booth and ordered a cold one, just making an effort to get acclimated. I tried to figure out where a pastor with a conservative theology might fit into the mix. I really didn't fit in at all, but after a few more cold beers, I didn't care. After the brief adjustment period, I realized that the bikers were on their way to Sturgis, and I had landed in the redneck capital of Wyoming on a Friday night. Yee-haw!

After I got a little more comfortable (drunk), I challenged a gentleman to a game of pool. The beer began to flow, the pool balls rolled, and I felt right at home—until something else caught my attention in a corner of the bar. I saw a man straddling another man as he proceeded to firmly place his fists repeatedly on the other man's nose and eyes. In other words, a biker was beating the hell out of a redneck.

My first thought was, *This must be normal behavior because nobody seems too alarmed, just like another day at the office.* But after further reflection, I thought, *Hell no! Not on my watch!* Under the influence of adult beverages, even an average man can become a blend of Superman, Godzilla and John Wayne.

With my best John Wayne strut, I headed to the corner to straighten out this minor altercation in short order. I had a long-neck bottle in my hand as defense. I'd never hit anybody with one before, but I had watched enough movies and thought I had a general idea of the way the procedure was conducted. As I walked, I felt a sense of empowerment that I was going to make things right. I would earn the respect of the victim in addition to receiving the Man of the Year Award from the other bar patrons.

That faulty reasoning only lasted for about two minutes.

I discovered later that the biker was from The Bandidos, one of the most notorious outlaw motorcycle gangs in the United States. When I confronted the gentleman, he immediately stopped the beating and got off the redneck he had pinned to the floor.

For a brief moment, I believed I had resolved the problem. I thought, *Well done! I handled that in a matter of fact way. That mean man knew better than to mess with the missionary man; I've got God on my side.*

As I was walking away, I heard a loud, explosive noise and felt the agonizing pain of a bottle of beer crashing against the side of my face. I turned around and saw what appeared to be a demonized rattlesnake, ready to strike. He had tattoos up and down his large arms and around his neck.

I had a feeling of helplessness, hopelessness, and fear as I began to do the Michael Jackson Moonwalk backwards. This was way above my pay grade; I knew I was way out of my league. Somehow, my enemy recognized that as well. Instead of attacking me in the same fashion as he had his last opponent, he simply snickered and sauntered out of the bar, looking over his back. He got on his bike and rode off. I believe this was God doing for me what I didn't have the sense to do for myself.

By the time the police arrived, blood was streaming down the side of my face. They insisted on taking me to the hospital to get my head sewn up, but I refused; I still had a little bit of macho left in me—not much, but a little. After stepping out of the ambulance, I got on my motorcycle and left. To go where? I didn't have a clue. All I know is that when I left the bar, the road led me to a hospital in Ft. Collins, Colorado.

Step Two in the Big Book of Alcoholics Anonymous reads,

"Came to believe that a Power greater than ourselves could restore us to sanity." It used to bother me when they read this step at AA meetings. Suffering from a serious case of inflamed pride and extreme stupidity, I would always say to myself, *Hey! Speak for yourself buddy! You might have taken the wrong road from reality, but my mind is perfectly intact. There is nothing insane about me!*

Let's put things in context—it had been less than one year since an eighteen-wheeler dodged my unconscious body sprawled on Interstate 40. At that time, I thought it was possible to be falling-down drunk, yet still crawl on my motorcycle and ride off safely. The only ride I ended up taking that night was a ride in an airplane as they life-flighted me to a hospital. Since I was so spectacularly successful in my last effort, why not try it again?

Once again, I must have been discovered on the side of the road by another motorist. My bike was covered with road rash, much the same way I was. My bike had no structural damage, so I didn't hit anything or anyone. I must have just passed out again.

My next memory was waking up in the hospital. I was told later that due to the severity of my head injuries, I had to be transported to the hospital in Ft. Collins from Cheyenne. When I came to, I had those familiar looking bandages on my head, arms and legs. The nurse said she needed to contact my closest relative. Although I understood what she was saying, I was unable to speak coherently due to the damage to my brain. I couldn't enunciate words; all I was able to do was mumble gibberish.

She retrieved a business card from my billfold and called Ann. The nurse explained to her that I had been in a serious accident and had severe head trauma, and that I couldn't talk or walk without assistance. She reported that it was too early to determine if the damage would be permanent.

It must have been horrific for Ann to imagine caring for a brain-damaged husband in addition to raising four young children alone. Many alcoholics have said, "My drinking doesn't affect anyone but myself." This rationale is a gross misconception. Such ignorant reasoning is motivated by our selfishness, hidden from our reality by our addiction.

Today I can see the effect it had on her; she was overwhelmed by feelings of fear, abandonment and betrayal. I had not only jeopardized my life, but I had also pulled the rug of security out from under her and then beat her with it. I had promised to never drink again, and I had lied.

With the help of physical therapy and by the grace of God, I was able to fully recover. Sometimes I still have a little difficulty formulating thoughts as quickly as I used to, and sometimes spelling really hard words like *dog* and *cat* gets the better of me. I also can't read as well as I could previously. The scars on the top of my head from the skull fractures resemble the shape of the state of Florida. In addition, my typing skills are up to about eight words a minute. All in all, things are pretty darn normal.

I was transported back to Phoenix, and that was the end of my career as a pastor. The embarrassment from the pastor being in another motorcycle accident, due to a drunken barroom fight over 1,000 miles from home, was more than the congregation could handle. The truth about my accident from the prior year came out as well. Their disappointment in me was justified.

They were hurt and angry, but the church wasn't willing to throw in the towel quite yet. With the support of the District Superintendent, Rick Penner, it was strongly suggested that if I wanted to retain my standing with the church, I would need to go a rehab facility in Fresno, California. The counseling organization's aim was to help Christian leaders rebuild their broken lives. The congregation was praying that I would face my addiction to alcohol and fully recover.

During the thirty days of treatment, it was common practice for me to slither out the door and go to the local tavern to relax after a long day of one-on-one counseling and group therapy sessions. I still wasn't convinced I was a real alcoholic; however, at times I did concede that I might have a slight drinking problem. I had tried explaining the situation in a way that only a real alcoholic could appreciate. I tried to convince the leaders in the church the reason I wrecked in Cheyenne wasn't because I was drunk, but because I was trying to be a good Samaritan. As an example, I cited the account in the scriptures where the other people passed by the man in the ditch. "But not me! I, too, stopped to help!"

The only difference was that in the process of trying to help, I had gotten beat up! I got hit in the head with a beer bottle, and it messed up my equilibrium. How could anyone ride their motorcycle safely under those circumstances? In other words, I was sent to the rehab facility for being a good Samaritan; that didn't seem right, did it?

My distorted way of thinking led me to believe I was being persecuted for trying to be a nice guy. In those days, it made perfectly good sense to me. The more I repeated the story, the more I believed it. The only problem was that no one else did.

Life Lesson #25: Distorted, irrational thinking can lead you to false feelings of persecution and emotional imbalance.

V

YOU MIGHT BE AN
ALCOHOLIC IF...

WHILE STILL HOLED up in rehab, I snuck out to attend worship services at a musty little bar I had found. I asked a fellow patron, with whom I had gotten fairly well acquainted, if he thought I might have a drinking problem?

His response was, "Hell, I don't know. What you are drinking?"

I said, "Rum and Coke."

"Doesn't sound like a problem to me."

His remark was made with such stern conviction—the voice of authority! I respected the gentleman's brilliance and intellect so much that I bought him a drink as payment for his insightful counseling session.

You might be an alcoholic if...while you're in rehab, you go to a bar to get advice about your drinking problem from another drunk. In the Big Book (the bible for drunks), it says on page 58, "it demands rigorous honesty" in order to find help. At this point in my life, I still wasn't willing to be honest. To admit I had a problem would demand that I do something about it; I wasn't ready to take action.

Life Lesson #26: You might be an alcoholic if while you're in rehab, you go to a bar to get counsel about your drinking problem from another drunk.

WHEN MY THIRTY days in rehab were over, I returned to Phoenix, certain that I'd resume my role as pastor. After all, I even had a letter from the psychologist in Fresno stating that he believed I was fit for leadership immediately. (I hadn't been honest with him either.)

On my return, I talked again with our district superintendent, Rick Penner. After a lengthy conversation Rick's final word to me was, "I don't think you're ready. I just don't sense any remorse."

I was appalled. What did he mean, I didn't have any remorse? My Harley was a total wreck! I was very remorseful about the condition of my bike.

Ann was still infuriated with me, and I was very remorseful about her attitude. My body still wasn't fully healed from the accident; I was very remorseful about the pain I had still had to endure!

After I made what I felt was a very compelling case, Rick dropped his head in sadness and said, "I'm sorry, Ron, but you are not getting it." I think he was actually saying, "I'm really sorry for you, Ron." He understood the gravity of my problem, but I was still missing the point. I still couldn't comprehend the depth and severity of my addiction.

Although I was able to manipulate the therapist into writing a letter of endorsement, I was unable to trick Rick. Initially, I thought he was just gently trying to put a drunken preacher out to pasture. But now I realize that both he and the congregation were still hoping I could be helped.

I was dismissed from my duties. It was a hard time. People in the congregation refused to return my calls, and when I'd run into someone I knew at the grocery store, they would ignore me or immediately turn and walk down the next aisle. I had hurt a lot of people, and their wounds were still raw. Their anointed one had fallen.

Still, I wasn't willing to let go of my drinking problem, nor was I willing to let go of the pastorate. Within the next few months I was a candidate at another church, but the congregation voted against naming me as their pastor. I think God told on me, or maybe they could sniff out a phony and picked up on my shallowness. If the congregation had selected me as their pastor, it wouldn't have taken long for me to start duplicating some of the same insane behavior from before.

Rather than getting better, I started getting bitter. I gave away thousands of dollars' worth of theology books, swearing to never darken the door of another church. I would teach those sorry SOBs a serious lesson about what an egregious error they had made! The church would suffer, maybe even on a nationwide basis, because they had rejected the Golden Boy. Instead of facing the gravity of my problem, I continued to blame others.

One of the most common ways to dodge responsibilities is to blame others for our misfortunes. It is a surefire way to never have to come to a healthy resolution.

Life Lesson #27: The best way to dodge your problems is to keep blaming others for your misfortunes.

THEN MY BROTHER told me about a salvage yard in southeast Kansas that was for sale. I didn't have a background in running a business like that, but I had started a rec center, a window washing business, and a church, so why not a salvage yard? With much persuasion, I convinced Ann to move to Kansas.

The next five years were characterized by instability—a roller-coaster ride on a continual decline. It turned out I really didn't know enough to run a salvage yard, so I closed it and instead opened a collision repair shop called The Edge. Living with my dad, I had grown up in a body shop so I had an element of experience. In time, I hired men who were far better than me at the work involved, and the business grew. We made a good living.

I have never known a real body man who didn't like to drink a few after work; the shop was the perfect environment to do so. My drinking habits still existed, but I tried to keep them well hidden. It was my common practice to watch the calendar for Ann's visits to her parents in Arkansas. She would take the kids, and I'd have the house to myself. I always looked forward to unrestrained drinking, since the rest of the time I had to be sneaky.

During one of my solo stints, I hit a highway guardrail and almost went off a bridge. I lied to everyone about what happened to the car. When a drunk's addiction grows, it's common that his morals go down the tubes. I continued to not to be honest with myself and others.

Life Lesson #28: As your addiction grows, your morals go.

WITH A BACKGROUND in working with young people, I soon noticed a need for a rec center, so I opened one and called it Studebaker's. We mounted the front-end of a '51 Studebaker on the wall and hooked up the headlights. The center was stocked with good-quality pool tables, foosball, shuffleboard, and video games. We even hosted local rock bands. In theory, it was a great place.

It was common practice for my oldest daughter, Megan, to open the center after school, and I would relieve her when I got off of work. That approach worked well until I started getting there later and later, with the stench of alcohol on my breath. I started bringing a large Styrofoam cup with me, filled with vodka. Within a year, the center closed. I told everyone it just lacked the financial backing, but in reality, I was simply not capable of offering guidance to others because I lacked the ability to guide myself or seek guidance from a loving God.

By this point, I had been abusing alcohol for years, and now Ann had finally had her fill. I had put her through hell. She told me unless I was willing to get help, her only choice would be for her and the kids to live a life without me in it.

I was stunned. Ann was a beautiful woman, a devoted mother, and we had been through so much together in twenty years of marriage. Doggone it, I was going to miss her!

The divorce was difficult on everyone, especially the kids. The night I left was a grim one. I remember packing my old car with a few items, and as I pulled out of the driveway, all four of the kids stood on the sidewalk waving goodbye with tears rolling down their cheeks. The small, knowing voice within was urging me to turn around, but the loud voice of alcohol was crying out at a much higher decibel. Sadly, I listened to the loudest voice. I still live with the shame of that choice every day.

In my spare time, I started restoring old cars. My oldest son had a '55 Chevy and Evan, the youngest, had a '65 Chevelle. They both still own them today. I purchased a '56 Chevy—a two-door delivery station wagon. We chopped the top, dropped it to the ground, installed lake pipes with flame throwers, and a stereo system that could be heard for a country mile. It was pearl white, but that wasn't quite enough. It needed a little more, like some ghost flames streaming down the sides. But no flames are better than bad flames, and I was afraid that if I painted them they would be bad, so I requested an accomplished artist do them for me.

Darren would come and work on the car for a while, and then not be seen again for a week or two. I was getting impatient with him. I tried to explain him to him that not only would my car not be complete, but my life wouldn't be either until I had those flames.

After another episode of me badgering him to work faster, he squared off with me and asked me a profound question. He said, "Ron, do you own this car, or does this car own you?"

It occurred to me that he was right. I had let the car represent much of my identity—who I was and what I stood for. I got the radical revelation that a lot of possessions from the past and present owned me. Our house in Phoenix with the four-car garage and a swimming pool owned me. Nice cars and motorcycles, they all owned me. They all represented who I was.

Jesus said, "Life does not consist of the abundance of what a man possesses." Somehow, I had overlooked that verse.

Life Lesson #29: You own your possessions; they do not own you.

A YEAR LATER, I was on my way to Sturgis again. My kids told me later, that they had had an eerie feeling that they would never see their dad alive again.

The ride had been superb—the mountains and plains were peaceful and serene at times. I had made several stops at the beer gardens to imbibe a few adult beverages on the way, but I was nowhere near the blackout stage of drinking, so I kept drinking. It was late at night, the moon was full, and the air was crisp. Riding conditions were perfect.

While traveling down the interstate near Sundance, Wyoming, I came across a deer standing in the middle of the highway—the worst nightmare of any motorcyclist. Terrified, I swerved to miss it, but the deer hit my front wheel. Before I even stopped skidding down the interstate, the small trailer I was hauling had landed on top of me, sandwiching me between it and the asphalt.

Again, I had injuries from head to toe. I hadn't been wearing a helmet, so the asphalt ground my head down to the skull. My foot was broken in four places, skin had to be grafted, and I lost the use of four tendons in my toes. Sound marginally insane? I thought so.

I had head injuries, road rash all over my body, and more broken bones. I spent about a week in the hospital, and they said I should stay longer until I told the doctor that I had no insurance, at which point he helped me pack my bag. My oldest son, Tyler, solicited the help of some friends, and came up to bring me and my bike back home.

When we went to the wrecker service where my bike had been impounded, I started inquiring about the other damaged bikes. "What happened to this guy?" I asked.

The manager said, "He ran off the road and died."

I asked in horror, "What happened to this guy?"

"He hit a deer and died."

I was overwhelmed with a sense of gratitude and guilt. *Why did they die and not me*

We took a brief tour of Sturgis, but it wasn't quite the same. I was with my eighteen-year-old son, and I was in a great deal of pain. Every time I hit a bump in my wheelchair, it was like someone hitting me in the chest with a sledgehammer. So much for beautiful women and badass bikes.

Even though I was in a wheelchair for a few months, I still managed to make it to the bar. At this time, I was living in a Winnebago RV I had paid a thousand dollars for. I think I paid too much. My humble abode was parked next to the body shop—it was a drunk's paradise. I drank daily, till late. I slept late, worked a little, and drank more. That seemed to be the regular routine.

One night, after a heavy session of drinking, I passed out in my RV. I had fallen asleep with a lit cigarette in my hand. When I woke up, the camper was filling with smoke. I immediately started dragging the mattress outside, but the flames caught the carpet on fire. In a drunken stupor, I was able to drop the mattress on the ground and stumble back in and extinguish the carpet.

When the smoke cleared, I moved to the spare bed and drifted back to sleep. I left the mattress resting in the grass for another month. It was obvious to others that my life was spiraling out of control but to me, it didn't seem to matter. Looking back, I attribute my survival solely to the love of God. The beauty of God's love shines the brightest in our darkest hours. When we are the most unloving, his grace is most pronounced.

Life Lesson #30: The beauty of God's grace shines the brightest in your darkest hours.

VI

A MORBID DEATH WISH

I WAS LIVING in dark times, and things were about to get darker. I rode my motorcycle hard and fast, and because of all the arrests for DUIs, motorcycle wrecks, and trips to the hospital, my brother suggested that maybe I had some sort of a morbid death wish. Little did he know that was exactly the plan. I hated life and everything about it with exception of four great kids. I hated what I had become; I hated myself and everything about me.

However, for my kids' sake, it wasn't quite time for my exit. I figured that if I could dodge death until I was 55, that age would be the best time. My father died at the same age, my youngest child would be eighteen, and kids would no longer need my substandard values influencing their lives. I viewed death as some view retirement—no more daily hassles like trying to conform to a lifestyle that made me miserable. I had lost my way and didn't know how to find it again, but if I could kill myself in a motorcycle accident, at least I could make my exit in the manner of my choosing.

But as life continued to take a downward spiral, I gave up on my 55th-year exit plan—55 was too far away, and I didn't want to bear the reality life had to offer that much longer. It occurred to me that if I were to hit a slow-moving train at a high speed, I would vanish like a bug on the windshield. It sounded plausible. It was nothing more than an effort to engage in a cowardly activity (suicide) that might be construed as an accident. However, everybody recognized that I was high risk and reckless, and they probably wouldn't have believed it.

For a practicing alcoholic, things will continue to worsen the longer our addiction is fed. Every day I wondered where and when my death would happen. Had it not been for the intervention of God via law enforcement, I have no doubt my plan would have been executed.

After leaving a bar late one night, my alcoholic girlfriend accused me of only having a three-speed transmission in my '56 Chevrolet. She claimed that I had been telling everyone it was a four-speed. She said that if I had four gears, I was skipping second. Not only had she criticized my car, but she had also insulted my intelligence and driving ability, and that did it!

I told her that if she wanted to see second gear, she should hold onto something and watch what came next. I dropped down to second gear while a tunnel ram fed the two four-barrel carburetors, bored .090 over. I started spinning my tires and going sideways from one side of the road to the other. The battle to save my ego was on.

In the midst of this latest exhibition of stupidity, I just happened to glance in my rear-view mirror and noticed some familiar blue flashing lights. When I pulled over, I was instructed to get out of my car and slowly place my hands behind my back.

Under the influence of alcohol, I always thought that I became better looking, bigger, badder, and smarter. If that were actually true, why would anyone leave a bar at 2:00 a.m. and be acting like that? Since then, I have been forced to rethink such faulty reasoning.

The officer informed me that I was displaying inappropriate behavior, and furthermore he was going to take me to jail. Little did I know that God would use the episode of flying gravel and smoking tires as a superb opportunity to give me time to contemplate my situation—in jail. I was granted an opportunity to think about ways to start living instead of simply creative ways to die. I did a few days in jail, which allowed me time to sober up and figure out my next step.

Life Lesson #31: You are granted the opportunity to think about ways to start living, instead of ways of dying.

LIFE LESSON 32

THE PRESSURE TO face reality or change my personality was getting greater, but I wasn't quite at the point to act on it yet. Rather than make any internal adjustments or hit a slow-moving train at a high rate of speed, I thought it would be better to relocate, hoping a new town in a new state would bring the serenity I was longing for. I sold the body shop and decided to move to Branson, Missouri. Branson is a tourist community with a reputation for being a comfortable family vacation spot. I wanted to believe that if I could alter my environment, my problems would vanish.

When I mentioned the idea to my friend Damon, his response was, "Don't forget, wherever you go, you will still be there." I had the misconception that by changing my environment externally, I would change internally. I didn't work that way for me.

Life Lesson #32: Don't forget, wherever you go, you will still be there.

I GOT a normal haircut like my brother Bob and got a job as a sales rep peddling vacation packages at a resort. The night before I arrived in Branson to begin my training, I was pulled over for speeding in Baxter Springs, Kansas, and charged with another DUI. I was sorry for the consequences but still not willing to admit I had a drinking problem.

The greatest sense of regret I had that night was having to watch the officer pour out a quart of Wild Turkey 101. While I watched from the back seat of the patrol car, I came up with the brilliant idea of breathing hard and fast, inhaling and exhaling heavily. My thought was that if I breathed heavily, the alcohol would dispense through my system before I could be officially charged.

If you ever get arrested for drunk driving, come up with another trick because my scheme only filled the policeman's car with the stench of cheap whiskey. When the officer got back in the car after pouring out my drink, he said, "Damn, it smells like the bathroom of a bar."

After being charged, I spent the night in jail, worried about the fact that I was supposed to be in Branson for training in only a few hours. Early the next morning, I managed to bond out and made it to Branson. It would have been terrible to get fired on my first day of work.

My legal advisors in the county jail had informed me that in their professional opinion, I was going to prison for a long time. My attorney was able to delay a court date, and I considered it an opportunity to drink until my impending doom.

While living in Branson, my daily routine consisted of stopping at The Pizzazz, a local bar, on my way home from work to "have just a few drinks" —the drunk's most famous slogan. Of course, it never happened that way; it seemed like a few minutes turned into a few hours, and few more minutes later they were announcing last call.

One of the loneliest feelings in the world was sitting at the bar alone, wondering how I got where I was, as well as how I was going to get home. It was a feeling of despair, depression, and fear. I had changed from wanting to drink to needing to drink.

My oldest daughter, Megan, came over from Arkansas to visit me. She was enrolled in college, preparing to be a counselor. We had been incredibly close earlier in her life. When she was a little girl, we would take walks in the park together, and when she was in elementary school, I visited her classroom periodically.

While we were living in Phoenix, Megan was our youth director's number one assistant. She had been blessed with a big heart and was always willing to serve. At the recreation center in Kansas, she worked for me as co-manager. We had always enjoyed a strong father-daughter bond.

Her visit to Branson for the weekend began with her calling me from her cell phone in tears. She was lost and was calling me from somewhere in Branson. Rather than offering to come and get her, I just gave her specific instructions on how to find the bar, since I knew the way very well. Somehow, I imagined she would enjoy her visit to the bar with me and other slobbering drunks.

By the time she found me, I was falling-down drunk, and her heart was broken, tears trickling down her soft cheeks as I continued to order more drinks. We stayed at the bar until she couldn't take it anymore. I stumbled out to my car and when I got home, I immediately drifted off to sleep. I thought it was great having my lovely daughter as a special guest, still unable to see what I was doing to her.

Throughout her young life, Megan had watched my standards steadily decline. The close relationship that I once had with my kids was much different now. I was drifting away to sea while my kids and other loved ones watching from the shore.

When I was a little kid, I had promised myself that I would never subject my kids to the misery I encountered growing up. But I had broken my promise and I was now living a full-blown lie. Ann had always told the kids that I loved them more than anything in the world, but now she had to alter the story and tell them the hard truth: "Your father doesn't love you more than anything. He loves alcohol more than anything."

I had illustrated this point perfectly when Megan came to visit me.

Life Lesson #33: You might be a drunk if you think your drinking doesn't affect others.

GOD in His love and grace sends teachers—sometimes in the form of law enforcement—to instruct us along the pathway of life. They are designed to act as hammers. The Great Sculptor sometimes uses parents, principals, employers, and the legal system to chip away our rough edges, forming us into works of art by His hand. In the beginning, we get light taps. If we are unresponsive, the size of the hammer tends to increase.

As my defiant behavior persisted, the strikes against my hard heart intensified.

It took every bad experience I ever had to form my character into the man God wanted me to become. Incidentally, the work still continues, but today I only require smaller hammers and lighter taps. The Master Architect intends for us to turn our experiences into building blocks. With those building blocks, we can create a shelter in which we can find peace. He longs for our spirit to get softer, willing to be molded into the image The Potter intended.

I was about to get struck by a very large hammer.

Life Lesson #34: The size of the hammer gets larger as your heart gets harder.

VII

THE MOMENT OF CLARITY DESCENDS

I WAS BEGINNING to have to deal with jail time for my DUIs. For one of the earlier DUIs, I had to do five weekends in jail. I could think of better things to do with my weekends, but nevertheless I counted myself as fortunate. I still wasn't to the point where I was willing to admit I had a problem. So, I continued to work and drink during the week in Branson and go to jail on weekends.

For my next DUI, I was sentenced to five straight days in jail. It was during this time that the lights started turning on, one by one. I was locked in a small ten-by-twelve-foot cell in Montgomery County, Kansas. It was almost unbearable and the silence turned it into a torture chamber.

Before my incarceration, I had created another type of prison which was characterized by being a slave to alcohol. But at least in those days, I was able to ignore its reality by keeping the music loud and the drinks strong. Things were different in jail. Every freedom I had ever known was now removed, except the freedom to think. And that was the freedom I wanted to escape the most.

The walls in my cell seemed to be covered with mirrors. My body seemed stained by shame, guilt, and all of the poor choices I had made that led me to my present destination. During those long days of solitude, I could clearly see when my problem started and where my romance with booze had brought me. Memories came flooding back about concerned friends and relatives who had tried to intervene, but I had never listened.

I was being forced to face the misery I had created for myself and others. I was only starting to see it, but it had existed over the course of my whole life. I felt like a jilted lover, being abandoned by alcohol.

During this time in jail, I wrote a poem entitled *Farewell Margarita*. It perfectly describes my love affair.

Farwell Margarita, for my love spanned three decades
We were always together, work,
Fun and hundreds of escapades

. . .

When you were next to me,
    I felt comfort and security,
    But for my family,
    All that you ever bred was fear, misery, and jealousy

Now I realize how blind I have been
    After thirty years of deception,
    This game has come to an end

The loss of beautiful homes,
    Many broken bones
    Hundreds of cuts and stitches,
    From Arizona, Kansas,
    And Wyoming ditches

Scars from head to toe
    God forgive me, once I started,
    I never seemed to say no

Innocent lives have been scarred forever
    Broken hearts tossed in the gutter

For over thirty years
    And a thousand shed tears
    You covered my heartaches
    And a multitude of fears

Today the thrill and excitement has died

False claims of happiness, advertisements on television and
magazines
  All of you lied

Goodbye Margarita to
  You and all your friends

You are cunning, baffling and powerful
  This relationship has come to an end

The feeling I experienced was like the calm right after a violent storm. There was wreckage and debris lying everywhere, but the storm that had lasted for thirty years was gone. A sense of peacefulness pervaded my soul as I stepped out of the delusion and denial. A heavy load lifted from my shoulders, and my spirit seemed to be saying, *Everything's going to be all right.*

I wrote a letter to my youngest daughter, Veronica, explaining that I was finally enjoying the most peaceful time I could ever recall in my entire life. I felt closer to God than I could remember. My days consisted of reading, meditation, and simply sitting alone in my serene little jail cell. It's peculiar how the darkest times in our lives can prove to be the most meaningful. I wasn't sure what my next step would be when I was released, but for that hour and that day, I didn't need to know.

Life Lesson #35: In the darkest hours come the most
meaningful experiences life has to offer.

I DIDN'T KNOW what the solution was, but at I least I knew what the problem was. It was me!

The day I walked out of jail, I felt the freedom from incarceration as well as an inner freedom and peace that had been missing for a few decades. When I took a breath of fresh air, I felt a release in my soul.

Part of my probationary requirements from earlier encounters with the law was to attend Alcoholics Anonymous meetings. At first, I was still stricken with a serious case of denial and pride. I felt like the guys in AA were just a bunch of dumbasses. What could a bunch of inbred hillbillies tell a man of my intellectual prowess that I didn't already know?

However, in another moment of clarity while locked up for my latest DUI, I looked through the tiny window in my cell and didn't see any of those hillbilly dumbasses—just other inmates walking around in circles like a bunch of monkeys. I realized that I was in jail, but none of my acquaintances from AA were. As I looked out of the small opening in my door, I wondered where they might be. Were they at home with their families? Or maybe at a Twelve Step meeting?

I immediately came to the obvious conclusion that I wasn't as smart as I thought I was, and the guys in AA weren't that dumb after all. During my first visit back to AA after getting out of jail, I loudly proclaimed to everyone how wise and insightful they had all gotten since the last time I'd seen them. Some of them didn't have a clue what I was talking about, but others did.

Life Lesson #36: Sometimes you come to see others as wiser than you first thought—especially as you begin to recognize the depth of your own ignorance.

AFTER MY RELEASE, my next stop after an AA meeting was to rush over to the house where Ann and the kids were living. I was excited to announce to my kids that their daddy had seen the light and realized he had a drinking problem, and I was going to quit.

For some reason, I expected them to throw their arms around me, shower me with hugs and kisses, call the mayor, and have a ticker tape parade complete with the high school marching band. That didn't happen. Instead I was met with skepticism. I caught a glimpse of my oldest son, Tyler, rolling his eyes at his sister Megan, as if to say, *Yeah, sure, Dad, we've never heard that story before!*

Even after I had 18 months of sobriety under my belt, my oldest daughter asked me with a heavy heart, "Dad, I've heard you say so many times that you were going to stop drinking, why should I believe you this time?"

My response was more honest this time than it had been in the past. I said, "I don't know, Megan. The only thing I can say is I feel like I have been to hell and back, and I don't ever want to revisit it again. I'm going to attend AA, and with the help of God, there's a chance I'll make it."

Most alcoholics don't realize how much trust and respect they have lost over years of deceiving others and causing them pain. In a sober state, I could see it plainly—written right on the faces of my children.

Life Lesson #37: If you've lived a lie, don't expect others to immediately believe you are telling the truth, even when you are.

EVEN THOUGH I attended AA on a regular basis, my heart wasn't always in the meetings; sometimes my attitude was blasé at best. I didn't always want to be there, and my self-righteous pride was still a stumbling block. But going to prison, landing in the hospital, ending up dead, or taking somebody else's life didn't seem like viable options, so I kept attending the meetings on a regular basis.

After attending meetings for about two weeks, I was approached by a tall, lanky Texan with a deep southern twang. Grant's leading remark was simple and to the point: "I've been attending these meetings now for about ten years, and I've seen a lot of people leave and only a few come back. Wanna know why some stay sober and many don't?"

With a disdainful attitude, I said, "Yes, please tell, the suspense is killing me."

Grant responded in a quiet, calm fashion. "The ones who keep coming back are the ones who have found a Higheeer Poweeer." His strong Texas accent made his last words into more syllables than should be allowed.

I asked him what Higher Power he was referring to. I asked him if he was trying to tell me that without the help of God, I wasn't going to stay sober. His response was calm and peaceful. With a slight smirk on his face, he simply responded, "I said this has been my observation. If you come up with a new way, good, go do it. And if it works, come back and tell me about your newfound formula."

I knew I had a problem, and I didn't have any new formulas—or even old ones—that seemed to pan out. In the past, I had made pledges that I would only drink on weekends. That didn't work because my weekends just got longer and longer, to the point where when one weekend was ending, the next was just beginning.

I had also tried making a commitment to quit drinking the hard stuff like whiskey and vodka, sticking with just beer, and maybe wine. But if you drink enough of the lighter stuff, you can still get falling down drunk and just as stupid; it just takes longer to get there. Nothing had worked for me.

Grant continued with his speech. "Just ask yourself how well you were doing managing your own life. In other words, if you had hired a fella to manage your life and you figured it was time for a job review, do you suppose you would give him a promotion or a demotion? If the results weren't that good, maybe consider hiring another manager."

I wouldn't have killed this imaginary guy I had hired to manage my life, but I'd have to hurt him badly—he'd really made a mess of things. My best intentions to manage my own life had led me and my loved ones down a long path of pain and misery. I was morally bankrupt. I had turned my back on God. It was like I had jumped bond and had been running from myself.

That brief conversation with Grant was the beginning of a long, meaningful spiritual journey. Asking somebody to be your sponsor is like asking someone to be your Valentine, and I asked him anyway. Grant asked me if I would be willing stay sober even if it meant losing my arm. What the hell was he talking about? I just wanted to stay sober and stay out of jail! And furthermore, which arm?

Despite those minor protests, I had to admit to myself that it was time to try something new. I hadn't been too successful at life in general; my family was gone and my career as a pastor had been flushed down the toilet. So why not be more serious about AA? What did I have to lose?

Grant led me through the Twelve Steps in a slow, methodical way. During this time period, my life began to take on a peacefulness that had been lacking for a long time. I knew I would have to go back to jail on one final DUI charge, but I felt relieved that it wouldn't have to be done alone; I had hired a new manager. I had reintroduced myself to my Higher Power.

My attitude toward work and my colleagues changed too. No more hangovers and wondering where all of my money went or what that woman's name from last night was, or why puke covered my shirt, and why the sheets were soaked with urine. I started associating with guys who were sober, laughing, and finding a new way of living.

In a few months I was forced to face further consequences for my fifth DUI. As I stood before the judge, I had mixed feelings. He only sentenced me to ninety days in jail, but I was still looking for a better deal. My attorney seemed to have taken a siesta in the midst of my sentencing; he didn't say a word. Rather than wake him up from dreamland, I decided to do my own lawyering.

I said, "Judge, I have a letter from a business in town that has offered me a job while I do my time." The judge looked at the letter, and immediately said no.

But I wasn't ready to give up yet, so I asked him if I could have house arrest. Another emphatic no. In one more last-ditch effort, hoping maybe he had forgotten I'd just asked him a few minutes earlier about work release, I calmly explained to him again that I had a promise of employment and a letter to prove it, and could I please have work release?

After a long pause, the judge looked at me with glaring eyes and responded, "Mr. Henderson, I feel like I have been very gracious with you. Your sentence could have been for a long time in prison. Go ahead and ask me *one* more time if you can have work release or house arrest."

I knew I had pushed him to his boiling point. I replied, "The carrot suit will be fine, judge. Thank you, judge."

Sometimes it's better to accept the reality that second best is the best. After I served my time and had some sobriety under my belt, I wrote a letter to the judge thanking him for the sentence he handed me. Jail had been tough for this sissy boy; I was grateful he hadn't made my punishment as severe as he could have.

God is much the same way. He is not interested in punishing us but rather in correction and discipline for the purpose of change. I had received a healthy spanking.

Life Lesson #38: God is not interested in punishing you, but rather in correction and change.

THAT TIME in jail proved to be ninety of the longest days of my life. If the doctor ever tells me I only have ninety days to live, I think I'll go to jail, just so it will seem like ninety years. I can recall overhearing some of the guys whispering to their friends that they saw me in the washroom, down on my knees, crying. I was sobbing for the heartache I had caused others, coupled with the fact I hated the long, dead-end road my drinking had led me down.

The saddest event of my prison time was the kids coming to visit me on Christmas Day. The only thing I could do was wear my best-looking carrot-colored jumpsuit and try to act as though I was doing great. In return, they would do the same. It was painful all around.

That time in jail keeps my life and my decisions in perspective. Alcohol no longer has the same draw for me.

I know friends who relapse. I always think, *What would I relapse to?* Wearing worn-out orange jump suits with hand-me-down underwear sporting brown skid marks that I didn't make? Would I want to relapse to another hospital, or maybe the morgue this time, due to another drunken motorcycle accident? The idea of a euphoric relapse had been smashed in the harsh reality of jail. Now, a relapse just doesn't sound that dang appealing.

Life Lesson #39: If you were to relapse, what would it look like? Would you be going back to a life of misery and shame? It doesn't sound that appealing.

AFTER RESTING for a while in the bed of self-pity, I decided it was time to make the best of a miserable situation. The court system didn't demand that I do my time with an attitude as pure as the wind-driven snow; they just demanded that I do my time, and anything beyond that would be up to me.

So it is in life—in many cases, we have no control over the cards that are dealt to us, like whether our parents were good or bad, or our race, or birthplace. It is our responsibility to maintain an appropriate attitude, a winning attitude toward adversity. I realized that making the best of less than perfect circumstances was up to me. If we hold to this principle, once the darkness has passed, we will be able to see how our misfortunes can benefit ourselves and others.

One of the disadvantages of being locked up all day was the lack of activity and exercise, especially for robust young men full of energy. Another brilliant idea: why not host the First Annual Montgomery County Jail Wrestling Tournament?

We moved all of the tables away, pulled cots off our beds, placed them on the floor, and the meet was on! After an hour or two, one of the guards came by and broke it up; we were informed that the activity was not permissible and were ordered to stop immediately. I always wondered what would have happened if we'd refused to obey. They couldn't throw us in jail because we were already there.

Up until we were rudely interrupted, we had a great time— muscles bulging; eyes squinting in the midst of hard, painful wrestling holds; sweat and a little bit of blood oozing from our pores. Since I was the promoter of the event, I thought it would be best for me to not participate. Instead I just officiated. (Never mind the fact that I was in my mid-forties, out of shape, and slightly overweight.)

After the event, everyone rested on the edge of their beds. The expression on their faces looked like they had conquered Mount Everest. It seemed as though they had returned to a normal part of society for a brief time. Some of the inmates said it was the best time they had ever experienced while in jail.

In addition to the wrestling tournament, we also hosted a spades and poker tournament. The first-place winner received their choice of two candy bars. Second place got one candy bar. Third place got an honorable mention. I called myself the Spade-ologist, but no one else found the title to be accurate.

I spent most of my days watching *Jerry Springer* and *Court TV*, reading, and meditating. Although I'd tried to make the best out of challenging situations, those ninety days were one of the most difficult times I can ever recall. But internally I was free, and eventually I would be released to a free world.

Most of all, I felt a freedom that I would never again have to be controlled by the dictates of alcohol. It was my prayer that alcohol would never gain control over me again and tell me how to spend my money or time or who my friends would be. That freedom was far greater than the freedom of leaving my jail cell.

I knew that once I was released, it wouldn't be easy or simple to get started on my new life. It was going to take work. But while I was locked up, I had a lot of time to think about where I previously had directed my energies. And I came to the conclusion that the big homes and nice cars I had sought were not any more satisfying than the false promises alcohol had made.

If all of the stuff had filled me, why had I still been so empty? Why had I needed alcohol to medicate my mind? I was aware that unless I changed my patterns of behavior and thoughts, I would be back on the same old dead-end road.

Life Lesson #40: Unless you change your patterns of behavior and thoughts, you'll be back on the same old dead-end road.

AFTER I COMPLETED my time in jail, my stepmother graciously allowed me to live with her. Make no mistake about it—not having a place to live, a car to drive or a job to work is not the best place to be. It had taken me a while to destroy everything around me, and it would take a while to build it back.

I straightened up the garage Dad had used as a body shop, and I contacted a few friends who owned car lots and started doing work out of that garage. My free time was spent attending daily AA meetings. In fact, AA turned out to be a healthy social outlet. I also started chopping the top off an '51 Henry J.

My spiritual life was slowly getting stronger as well. The little body shop was providing an adequate income, and my life was simple and serene.

During the nine months I lived with my stepmother, I worked with other alcoholics. It was similar to the days when I was a new Christian; I wanted every drunk in the world to know the feeling of this newfound freedom I had. The experience had been powerful in my life, and I wanted to share this hope with others. The feeling of fulfillment was so great that I wanted to do it all the time.

In the fall of 2002, I loaded all of my belongings in my old Corvette and headed back to Branson. My new job was similar to the one I had when I was living there the first time: working in the resort business selling vacation packages. The sales managers reminded us constantly that our incomes could and should be in the six figures. But I didn't feel the need for six figures. I had chased that rabbit before and when I'd caught him, he wasn't that tasty.

Furthermore, most of the folks who came to the resort couldn't afford the vacation packages we were offering. They came to sit through our pitch so they could receive a free ticket to see a local entertainer. If they had the resources to begin with, they more than likely wouldn't be subjecting themselves to a high-pressure salesperson. I decided to look for something else instead of the promise of a six-figure sales job.

I explained the dilemma to my sponsor, Grant, and he recommended I apply at a drug rehabilitation facility. He said he knew some people there and could help me get my foot in the door. Working at the center was confirmation that I wanted to devote the rest of my life to helping other drunks and junkies.

Life Lesson #41: We chase the rabbit of glitter, glamour, and money, and when we catch it we are still empty and hungry.

VIII

WHY WORK WITH
DRUNKS AND JUNKIES?

HAVE you ever wondered why Jesus spent his time with the less-than-respectable members of society? Was it because he needed friends and they were the only ones who would associate with him? Was it because he didn't have a high school education, or maybe because he didn't have a steady job and an impressive port-folio? Or was it because they were hungry, tired, thirsty, depressed, demoralized, wounded, broke, bewildered, and confused...

Jesus accepted them as they were, without a hidden agenda. Luke 15:1 says, "Dishonest tax collectors and notorious sinners often came to listen to Jesus." They were at ease with Him; He embraced them in their sad state with no judgment or ridicule. The rest of society thought of them as human debris.

Why would I want to work with drug addicts and alcoholics? For many reasons. If Jesus was walking the earth today, I believe his ministry would be aimed at this population as well as other unfortunate segments of our society. They have been beat up, burnt out, and are bedraggled seekers, looking for the missing pieces of life's puzzle. Addicts and alcoholics have suffered huge economic losses, been rejected by family and friends, and are often haunted by an abundance of legal problems. They have lost their social standing and long for a small taste of self-respect and a return to some form of dignity. Chemically dependent people are often at a place in life where guilt and shame are constant compan-ions, and they desperately need grace and forgiveness. I speak from firsthand experience.

It is a superb place to reach in life when we are forced to cry out for help. "Blessed are those who hunger and thirst for right-eousness, for they shall be filled," states Matthew 5:6. The plea-sures of this life have left addicts longing for serenity, and in many cases, they don't know where to go for insight or assistance. For years, they have chosen to live in silent misery, carrying their burdens alone. To openly admit that they have been dominated by a substance that is leading them down a path of destruction is profound.

The final path down the road of surrender brings peace and rest. All of the broken relationships, fractured hearts, and failures, both professional and personal, have left them empty. The crutches that they leaned on are weak and broken. A broken, empty addict reaching out for help in his or her greatest need can find meaning and purpose in life.

Many people never discover the beauty of failure and misery. But in my own life, some of the most meaningful experiences have come not from financial gain, educational accomplishments, or prestigious positions, but rather during the loneliest, darkest moments.

Adversity and pain have become great teachers and even, in a peculiar way, friends. They have reconnected us to ourselves and taught us much as we fail and fall into the loving arms of our Father God. If we can learn and gain insight from our mistakes and failures and use our life experiences to encourage others, we have hit upon one of the ultimate purposes of life.

Life Lesson #42: Adversity and pain can become great teachers and, in a peculiar way, even friends.

THE ONLY DISADVANTAGE of working in a rehab facility was that the entry-level wage didn't align with my financial obligations, which weren't entry-level. I had fines to pay, probation fees, and I was trying to help Ann with the kids. I felt that if I were going to be able to do this type of work full-time, it would necessitate earning some credentials. Many of my friends told me I was too old to go back to school; others said that due to my head injuries from the motorcycle accidents, I wouldn't be able to keep up with graduate level courses. Still others insisted that the cost would be prohibitive.

I'm not a King David, but I do recall that some of his critics suggested that he was not capable of taking on Goliath. If he could complete such a task with God's help, couldn't I go back to school, also with the help of God? In some cases, it's best to press forward in faith, despite the advice of well-meaning friends.

I never considered myself particularly bright or academically-minded, but I have been able to muster the strength to persevere under harsh circumstances and not give up. My next steps forward would be some of the most mentally demanding and difficult I've experienced over the course of my lifetime. God would be my strength.

Life Lesson #43: In some cases, it's best to press forward in faith, despite the counsel of well-meaning friends.

AFTER CONSIDERING SEVERAL SCHOOLS, I selected John Brown University in Siloam Springs, Arkansas. It was a faith-based school where I wouldn't feel the need to defend the existence of my Higher Power. As it turned out, my friends were right in every one of their reasons I should not go back to school; my "advanced" age coupled with my major head injuries would definitely make it an uphill battle. But I was determined to do it.

Because of my many accidents, in which I'd had my head slammed into the asphalt several times—without the protection of a helmet—some of the grey matter that used to be in my skull had been left behind back on the highway. That meant I had to study twice as hard to get grades half as good as my classmates.

But the biggest hurdle would actually prove to be finances. I knew I would need a job that had some flexibility in the hours. It also needed to be a job that provided enough resources to allow me to stay afloat.

Life Lesson #44: You can teach an old dog new tricks, if he is hungry enough.

EVER SINCE THE days of starting the recreation center and living in the loft of the building and out of the back of my car, I have learned to adapt to many situations. With a background in collision work, it seemed like a good idea to open another body shop. I found a nice building just across the state line in Pineville, Missouri. It had formerly been a tire store, but now it was just sitting vacant in an excellent location.

I was able to negotiate a deal: I would take the building on the stipulation that the owner would allow me to live there. He had trouble at first trying to understand why I would want to live in a rat-infested metal building that got extremely hot in the summer and very cold in the winter. But after I explained that it was out of necessity, not preference, he understood and consented. The shop would provide a means of making money while I was in school and offered the extra bonus of providing a place to live when I didn't have the funds to pay rent for a house.

Living in the shop proved to be another one of those character-building experiences. Even the small stuff, like going to bed, provided challenges. If I forgot to take off my shoes before I turned the light off when I went to bed, I could be certain to get jolted with 110 volts, due to faulty wiring. And once I got into bed, it was a signal for the rats and mice to start partying. As they held tag-team wrestling matches and dance parties on the Styrofoam ceiling, I would yell obscenities at them, but it never seemed to deter them.

Celebrating Christmas with my kids in a body shop was better than doing it from a jail cell, but not much. Nevertheless, we made the best of it.

One year, we decided to have a bowling tournament. But instead of going to the bowling alley like most normal families, we designed our own bowling alley in the body shop. I should have patented the idea. We gathered logs used for the wood burning stove as pins. They were about one and a half to two feet in length. Rather than using a bowling ball like I've seen a lot of folks do, we improvised with a basketball. The cold, drafty metal building forced us to keep moving in the dead of winter. But the kids and I had the time of our lives as the logs and basketball banged repeatedly against the metal door.

I have to admit it wasn't an ideal situation, but I believed that eventually the tide would turn, and things would be different. When friends asked me where I lived, I just mumbled quietly and vaguely about my living conditions. I believed God led me back to graduate school, and I believed he would use my failures in life to be a source of encouragement to others. And in the meantime, nothing would be handed to me on a silver platter. Instead, I got a steady diet of Ramen noodles and bologna.

It seems like these days, we suffer from an epidemic of fixation on immediate gratification. We buy cars and homes we can't afford; our kids receive money without producing any effort for it. They demand the latest video games and designer clothes. Do we indulge them because we never had that stuff when we were kids? Is it that we would rather have their friendship than their respect? Eventually, they have to face the real world, and they struggle because accomplishment requires hard work and determination.

This is a foreign concept to many of our young people in society today. But it pays to learn that hard work is a part of a successful life. I embraced this truth during this period in my life, working hard to build a future for myself.

After four long years of studying, I received a Master's in Community Counseling and was eligible to become a Licensed Professional Counselor. It had been a long journey, but it seemed that the sacrifice would be worth it.

After graduation, I accepted a job as a therapist for mentally-disabled pedophiles in Sallisaw, Oklahoma. For obvious reasons, this segment of the population is among the most hated and disrespected in our society. It wasn't the position of drug and alcohol counselor I ultimately hoped to hold, but I was broke and hungry and needed to find work.

When I was in school, one of my professors made a remark in class one day that I'll never forget: "Before we become too critical and judgmental of others, just remember that if what has happened to them had happened to you, perhaps you'd have done the same as they have." I'm certainly not justifying their behavior, but most of us have never faced some of the horrendous experiences they have endured. In some cases, they were pimped out for drugs by their parents, and they were taught at a young age that it was permissible to engage in such activities.

Regardless of inborn ethics, God's standards, social norms, or the laws of our land, the barrier to reality and remorse seemed impossible to overcome, which would explain why most of them were either locked up in prison or under professional care for the rest of their lives. I was told on numerous occasions that I was the first person who ever showed them any form of respect. There is a difference between endorsement and respect, of course. I never condoned but I never condemned.

I felt in my heart that God was not calling me to serve this clientele forever. At the time, I was living in a small town in Oklahoma and I was praying that He didn't want me to live there for the long haul. It was a nice place to visit, but not a fun place to live. I have always preferred the warmer climates and always dreamed of living close to the water.

It felt odd, however, when an opportunity presented itself that would actually allow me to relocate. Part of my job duties allowed me to work with young people who had a variety of disorders, and one client of mine had been blessed with a very attractive mother named Angela. Late one night I got a call; Angela was on the other end of the line.

Initially, I thought there must be some sort of serious trauma going down on the home front. But after hearing Angela's voice, I realized that was not the case at all. Her voice sounded like a kitty cat purring in my ear, or like soft velvet. She requested permission to come by my house and give me a good-night kiss.

I had noticed a mutual attraction between us the first time she came to my office. Although nothing was ever said, the momentum and excitement had continued to build. Her beautiful, dark eyes drew me to her. Of course, I tried to maintain my professionalism, but on the inside, I was like clay and she was the potter, molding my heart with every smile and glance. I was interested in her, to say the least, and I knew she was interested in me.

Though I was a busy man with a tight schedule, I thought I would surely have time to squeeze in a kiss or two. Angela's soft lips melted my heart, and I was like Jell-O as I innocently held her to me. I gave her a final good-night kiss and wished her well, already missing her the minute she walked out my door. I wondered how soon it would be before I could see her again, if ever.

I knew the ethics code pertaining to my clients, but this situation was not a dual relationship because Angela was not my client; her child was. At least that's what I tried to explain to my work colleague Brian the next day. I felt like I was going to an accountant, asking them to help me find a loophole in the tax system.

When I sought the advice of Brian, he started treating me like a mentally-disabled person. Rather than agree that there was no clause regarding such behavior, he considered it his ethical responsibility to report it to my supervisor. My accountant had turned me in to the IRS instead of helping me with that legitimate deduction.

The next day, I was told that I had the option of either resigning or being fired. As I cleaned out my desk, I was heartbroken that nothing could ever materialize between Angela and me, not to mention that I was also now unemployed. I had violated the ethics code for professional counselors, and my termination was immediate. I never did have the opportunity to see Angela again. At that point, I knew what I did was wrong, and I didn't feel the need to dwell on it.

Before the day was over, I pulled out my ragged Rand-McNally Road Atlas and started dreaming. When unexpected circumstances arise, we can wilt, blame others, and hate ourselves. But it's better to begin looking for a solution instead of sulking about the circumstances. I don't feel that I have been endowed with a lot of great talents or strengths, but my ability to dream is still alive and well.

Life Lesson #45: When unexpected circumstances arise, you can wilt, blame others, or hate yourself. But it's best to begin seeking a solution instead of sulking about the circumstances.

I WAS INTRIGUED with a little section of the map called Gulf Shores, Alabama. I had to squint to see it, but the tiny dot on the map met all my criteria: it was close to the water, and I knew the weather would be more accommodating. My research had just begun, but my excitement was building. Within a few days, I gassed up my motorcycle, strapped a tent to the back of it, and took off for a Gulf Shores vacation.

Like a five-year-old leaving for his first day of school, I was full of fear and excitement. I recalled an expression my ex-father in-law often used: "I have lived a life of no regrets." Well, unlike him I had many regrets regarding the past, but I didn't want to let the past dictate my future. I didn't want to finish the final quarter of the game of life looking back and wishing I had done what my heart had beckoned me to do. The trip down to Alabama was very educational, to say the least.

As I rode through Arkansas, Louisiana, and Mississippi, I was reminded that a lot of folks still hadn't gotten over the days of slavery and cruel discrimination. When I stopped for gas and asked to use the restroom, one of the employees politely told me that I couldn't because it was out of order.

But while I was filling my tank, the restroom must have been repaired because just then a black gentleman walked out the bath-room door. I got a brief glimpse of how they must feel in parts of our country where pockets of hate and discrimination still exist. At the same place, I asked how far the Mississippi state line was, and nobody knew. It's possible that they had never been out of the community, much less the state.

As I rolled into Alabama, I noticed the license plates read Sweet Home Alabama. In a way, it did feel like I was entering my new home, and it was sweet! I don't recall any license plates that read Sweet Home Oklahoma, Kansas, Arkansas, Missouri, Illinois, Nebraska, or Arizona. That was enough confirmation for me that I was in the right place. As I arrived in Gulf Shores, I felt the same way the Israelites must have felt as they entered their promised land. Even though there were giants, it was still paradise compared to where they had come from.

I set up my tent in a campground nestled next to one of the inner coastal canals. It would be a great place to sit and meditate in the morning before setting out on my journey to look for some land.

People at the campground warned me about a wandering pet pig that had a reputation for relentlessly trying to get into tents. I have heard of bears in Colorado, lions in Wyoming and Montana, and Arkansas has their razorbacks; so maybe Alabama had their pigs.

Actually, I thought the guys at the campground were pulling my leg—until I woke up one morning with a large pot-belly pig trying to get in bed with me. After I realized I wasn't having a nightmare, I got up, kicked the pig in the rump a few times, and she sauntered off to annoy someone else. The owner told me they got her when she was just a tiny baby, and everyone in the campground adopted her and fed her too much too often. The lady explained that it would be best if I avoided feeding her. I politely said, "Yes ma'am, you won't have to tell me twice."

Visiting a tourist community hundreds of miles away from my network of sober friends was risky business for a real alcoholic like me. To compensate, one of the first things I did was look up where AA meetings were held. Some AA meetings were better than others, but I've never been in a bad one. AA has a unique formula that allows a complete stranger to walk in and feel totally at home; Gulf Shores and Orange Beach were not any different.

I wish the traditional church was able to capture the beauty of being open and accepting of one another like AA can. Most of the meetings I have attended are characterized by the ability to admit our failures and share how God has delivered us from our personal road to hell. AA has learned some sound biblical principles to help make their program successful; the church could learn something from them. Perhaps churches today could shift directions and begin emulating the Twelve Step model, which is illustrated by openness and admission of faults, rather than the pseudo-phoniness that is all too prevalent in many congregations.

In the brief time I attended meetings in Gulf Shores, I always left with a feeling that I had known some of those folks for decades instead of just a few weeks. This has been my experience in AA meetings all over the country.

Another thing I loved about Gulf Shores was its natural beauty. Gulf Shores is said to have some of the whitest sand in the world. I'm not sure what the significance of that is, or who did the research, but somebody supposedly has. I spent a lot of time doing my own research.

The view from the fishing pier was breathtaking; I often looked out at the magnificent ocean at dusk, imagining its power and might. I could see its natural splendor. Though I didn't know for sure how deep it was, I knew it was massive and powerful enough to swallow me like a whale would a minnow.

I enjoyed talking to the fisherman and listening to their tales about catching sharks and barracudas. As I was walking along the pier one night, I watched a sting ray flop around on the deck as everyone stood and watched in amazement. At the same time, a shark and a red snapper were being reeled in. The fisherman carefully unhooked the sting ray, and the beautiful creature slithered back into the ocean with elegance and grace.

The experience of seeing a small part of God's creation cost me nothing; I just happened to be there. But the feeling was priceless. I felt like a speck of sand next the powerful ocean. It put my place in the universe into perspective.

On one occasion, another biker who lived at the campground asked me if I wanted to ride to "Florabama" to cash in his lottery ticket. I neglected to ask him what Florabama was; in Oklahoma, lottery tickets are sold in convenience stores, so I thought it was something similar. But I soon found out that Florida did it differently.

It turned out that Florabama was a historical biker bar, right up alongside the beach, with at least fifty Harleys parked outside. Unlike the guys who trailer the bikes to a location, put on their new leathers, and then take a short ride before going back to their hotel for a nap, these guys appeared to be real bikers. They had tattoos up and down their arms, and scars and wrinkles covering their faces. Most of them looked like they'd lived a hard life.

I didn't pack a lot of clothes when I'd left Oklahoma, so I counted myself fortunate when I found a pair of shorts on the beach one previous night. I never figured out why they were left there, but I washed them and started wearing my recycled, funky-colored beach shorts with a Hawaiian shirt. The combination worked just fine in Gulf Shores...but not when we rolled into Florabama.

As I walked up to the bar and ordered a Coke, I could feel the stares of the hardened bikers as they tried to figure out if I was a representative of the Rainbow Coalition, maybe having taken a wrong turn somewhere and ending up in their bar by accident. It had been over eight years since I had been in an establishment of this nature, let alone one that was hundreds of miles from home. The last time had been in Cheyenne, Wyoming, where I'd been drunk, gotten a beer bottle busted on the side of my head, crashed my bike, and ended up in the hospital with a skull fracture, ultimately losing my position as pastor. This time was going to be different, doggone it.

My buddy gave me a tour of the facility. One spectacle I vividly recall were three long ropes reaching from one end of the bar to the other. Each strand of rope was covered with three or four layers of bras. I decided that it was about time for this long-haired country boy to find the nearest exit before the sun went down and the old Ron reemerged alive and well and possibly ended up dead this time. I could imagine that a person could easily catch something in there that even Ajax couldn't wash off, not to mention how her boyfriend, a probable graduate of Florida State Prison, might feel as I tried to romance his woman.

So, after I drank my Coke and took the tour, I left the bar peacefully. I was grateful to be sober, and grateful that I was no longer controlled by a substance more powerful than myself. The memories started to come back...

The lonely nights spent trying to find comfort and meaning in a cold beer and a shot of whiskey were still fresh in my mind. Waking up the next day, feeling like a thousand Russian soldiers had walked through my mouth with their socks on, my head pounding like a marching band with the bass drum slamming against my skull. Wondering what I'd said to somebody that made them feel it was necessary to give me a black eye. Wondering why there was dried blood on my shirt. Or those times when I just fell asleep in a parking lot after wandering around looking for my car. Where did the pocket full of money go? Did I loan it to someone, or did I buy everybody at the bar drinks and borrow some more after I'd spent it all?

But they were all just memories. On this occasion, at Florabama, I was proud to get back on my motorcycle, wearing my funky recycled shorts and a funny colored shirt, humbled that God had given me enough grace to escape the grasp Hell once had around my throat with the aim of extinguishing my life.

A few days before I left town, the kind folks at the employment office walked me through the process of looking for work opportunities. I filled out some job applications and spent the next few days riding up and down the beach, hanging out on the pier, and staying out of bars.

I headed back to Sallisaw, Oklahoma on a Friday, not knowing where I was going to work, but knowing where I wanted to live: Gulf Shores, Alabama, just a few miles below heaven. A home, a little money, and a job were I all I needed. When I arrived back in Sallisaw, I decided that if necessary, I would take only what I could pack on my bike, selling the rest of my possessions and hitting the road.

Immediately I started planning for my move. But as adventuresome as I thought I was, I found there were things I had become attached to—photo albums of the kids, a few books, and some clothes. I was going to have to sell the motorcycle and my low-rider pickup and buy something more functional. If I was able to make a decent profit, I could leave town with enough money to live on while I was seeking employment. Fortunately, the sales went well, and I found a Ford Ranger pickup for a thousand dollars and started packing.

A few days before I was planning to leave, I received a phone call from a mental health agency in Gulf Shores that I had interviewed with while I was down there. They explained that their organization was an intensive outpatient drug and alcohol facility aimed at treating convicted federal and state parolees. They asked if I would be interested in accepting a position as a therapist.

After the conversation was over, I had to pause, pinch myself, and ask if it was real. Did she say I was going to be working with junkies and drunks as a counselor, living on the Gulf Coast?

I interpreted this conversation as a wink from God that everything was going to be all right. That would prove to be only one of several winks from my Lord. Sure, I would miss the great state of Oklahoma, the blustery winters and the flat land, but I was confident that I would somehow eventually make the adjustment to living near the ocean. The position paid less than 45 percent than what I was accustomed to making, but I felt a divine calling to work with this population.

I also had a deep-seated desire to pay back God (and others who have helped me) for showing me a better way of life. I learned valuable skills from an accumulation of years of failure that qualified me for the position—these courses couldn't be offered in grad school. As I left town, I sensed a new chapter of my life was about to begin, and I felt an eager sense of anticipation and excitement similar to the feeling I got when I stole my first kiss from Kathy Morrow at the age of five.

As I drove into Arkansas, leaving Oklahoma behind, I decided to stop and see all of my kids before I left. I pulled into the collision shop that my oldest son Tyler managed. As he stood out front with some of his employees, they watched my truck pull up. It was packed to the brim, with stuff hanging off the sides.

"That guy looks like a refugee from the Beverley Hillbillies," Tyler told one of his friends. He didn't know it was actually his dad, on a mission from God.

During my visit, we both had an eerie feeling that I was moving far away, and we didn't know how long it would be before we saw each other again. We tried to enjoy each moment. I knew I would be back in a few months, since Megan was about to give birth to her first child—my only grandchild. Nevertheless, it was a bittersweet visit. After a few days, I said goodbye and headed south.

As I entered the city limits of Mobile, I had feelings of excitement and fear of the unknown. I headed east on I-10, and my heart began to pound. The beauty of this region had a powerful draw on me, and while it didn't completely remove the fear, it certainly made the move easier. Driving over the bay with the ocean on either side of the road made me feel as if I was moving into a sacred land. I felt like Moses when God told him to remove his sandal, because he was standing on holy ground.

I found a clean, cheap room for the night. I hadn't left Oklahoma with a lot of money, so I couldn't live in a motel too long. Within a few days, I came to the conclusion that living in Gulf Shores would not be realistic. The distance to Mobile was a bit too far—almost an hour each way. Several of my friends recommended Daphne, Alabama. It was right on the eastern shore and still within thirty minutes from work. Living in Daphne would get me out of Mobile, the city with the second-highest murder rate per capita, right behind New York City. In Daphne I would still be minutes from the beach.

I believe most people never experience much adventure, excitement, or success in life because of fear and a lack of faith. Our God is too small, or our God is us. Recently one of my clients approached me with an acute sense of fear and gloom.

"Everything is going all right. It's just that out of the blue, I am consumed with an overwhelming sense of fear," she confided to me. "I start feeling like everything is going to fall apart."

"If everything depended upon us, we should be afraid," I told her. "But if everything depends upon God, we have nothing to fear. Fear is the most common enemy of happiness."

Life Lesson #46: If everything depends upon us, we should be afraid. But if everything depends upon God, we have nothing to fear.

I started scouting out the land around Daphne. At one point, I pulled in the parking lot of a fast-food restaurant with the classifieds in my right hand and a greasy piece of chicken in my left. I bowed my head and prayed.

Dear Lord, you know I don't have much money, and what little I do have is running out quickly. I know you own the cattle on a thousand hills, so I am asking that the first number I call be The Place. Not only that, but I would like to be close to water. I'm asking for someplace that has an element of privacy, away from the party crowd. I can't afford much. I need your help. Oh, and thanks for the greasy piece of chicken. AMEN.

God is my witness; the first number I called was an elderly woman. She told me about her little cottage, a property right on the eastern bay. Someone was already interested in the place, but she had lost his number and was waiting for him to call back. Also, the lower level of the cottage was being remodeled and wouldn't be finished for a few months. She offered to take my number, however, and if she didn't lose it, she would call me back when it was done. Or, she suggested, I could keep her number and call her back to take a look at it in a few months.

I hung up the phone, ate another piece of chicken, and paused. Wait. She lost the number and was waiting for the other guy to call her back? What if she didn't ever hear from him again? I called her back and asked if the gentleman had left a deposit. She said he hadn't, but he was supposed to come by and look at it, and if he liked it, then he would leave one.

"Well, Ma'am," I said in my most respectable voice, "I am here, and if I like it, I will leave a deposit today!"

The kind old woman then explained that she was on her way to Orlando and didn't expect to be back for a week—another roadblock. There was no way I could spend another week in a motel and still have enough money left for a deposit.

"If I could just look at it, when you get back, I'll settle up with you," I suggested. She said that wouldn't work because the place was locked, but if I wanted to drive by and if I liked it, maybe she could get her daughter to give me the key.

"Don't forget to walk down to the beach," she reminded me. That was like saying sic 'em to a dog.

I cranked up my little four-cylinder, five-speed Ford hillbilly truck, with junk still hanging off the sides, and rushed over to the property. As I drove down the desolate road toward the house, I felt like I was revisiting the movie set of Deliverance. The area was actually a multimillion-dollar neighborhood; the elderly woman's property just seemed a little out of place. In the midst of the upper-crust, ritzy crowd was a real, live, redneck domicile just like what I would have expected to find in the back woods of Arkansas.

Tall pine trees hung over the long drive and surrounded the entire property. When I pulled up in front of the cottage, it was love at first sight! The cottage had a light-yellow exterior, with a huge porch complete with swing and comfortable easy chair. I counted over fifteen unrestored cars sitting around. Some were vintage: her husband owned two '55 Fords, a '56 Crown Victoria, and numerous older Mustangs. They were all right out in plain sight so God and everyone else could look at them, whether they wanted to see them or not. I just knew that this was my new home.

I could easily see the bay adjoining the property right through the trees. I walked down to the water to inhale the fresh ocean breeze. To my right, I could see downtown Mobile. The buildings seemed to represent our daily responsibilities and the place that would demand my attention for the purpose of survival. To my left were endless miles of water that beckoned with freedom and adventure.

I dropped to my knees in the sand and asked God to help me not ever get so caught up in the daily hustle and bustle of life that I would lose my quest for freedom and adventure. I thanked Him for giving me more than I had ever imagined.

Life Lesson #47: Sometimes it's good to drop to your knees and ask God to help you avoid getting so caught up in the daily hassles of life.

As I WALKED across the lawn toward what I knew would be my new home, I felt my Heavenly Father's love for me, even in small matters such as living conditions. I went inside and took a look around, then went back outside again. Like a gold miner, I staked my claim by unloading everything I owned onto the front lawn. I thought it would be too presumptuous to immediately occupy the house without getting authorization from the landlord, but within my heart, I knew the deal was done.

That afternoon, I called the owner and explained that I wanted the cottage on the bay. Since one of the only landmarks I was familiar with in town was Kentucky Fried Chicken, she arranged for her son-in-law to meet me in the parking lot so I could give him the deposit. The chicken place seemed only fitting, since it was there that I found the ad and made the call regarding the property. This called for a celebration—another piece of greasy chicken!

The next day, I moved my belongings into the house. When I was done, I had to laugh at the simplicity of my furnishings.

My computer was set up on an old card table that used to belong to an ex-girlfriend. My Sanyo television with a bad speaker was on a small entertainment unit that I gotten from another ex-girlfriend. She had actually given me the entertainment unit; the card table was a different story. That ex-girlfriend had loaned it to me for a moving sale. I have often thought about mailing it back, if only she would return my digital camera.

My dining room table belonged to Cynthia, my landlord. It was set up under a tree in the front yard—a small table with a glass top and four matching chairs, each with a red and white checkered cushion. I also had a love seat in excellent condition that matched perfectly. It, too, was donated by an ex-girlfriend. She'd had a lot of money, a large home, and not quite enough space for everything she owned; she gave me her leftovers.

My most prized possession, though, was a gift from Megan that she had given to me when I finished grad school. It is a picture of trees on a foggy day, surrounding a small bridge which leads off into the unknown. It perfectly illustrates the beauty of life, full of mysteries and challenges, fear and excitement, all encompassed by a loving God who will never leave us as we adventure into strange lands. The picture seemed very appropriate for this day as I moved into a new space and a new phase in life.

The bedroom was even more simply furnished: a queen-sized air mattress resting on a 1940-style frame, also compliments of Cynthia. On the wall hung a large, hand-painted picture of "The Dude in the Stude." It's a painting of a '51 Studebaker with a gentleman standing next to it, wearing a sports coat. He has a long, chest-length beard, and bears a slight resemblance to Billy Gibbons, the singer for ZZ Top. An artist painted the picture for me when I started the recreation center called Studebaker's.

On the opposite wall hung a painting, by the same artist, of a '56 Chevy wagon with a chopped top. The wagon sported side pipes with flame throwers, a wild red paint job, and a tunnel ram bulging out of the hood. I owned a car similar to it in the late '90's. The only other item in the bedroom was a dresser. The drawers were a little tricky to open sometimes, and it definitely wasn't the prettiest dresser on the block, but it did the job. It was given to me by my ex-wife Ann.

The bedroom also had a huge walk-in closet. I never could understand the logic of putting such a large walk-in closet in a two-room cottage, but doggone it, I had one and I was proud of it!

I spent an hour or so moving things in and arranging my new home before taking a break. As I rested on the sofa, I realized that over the years I had taken a downward-spiraling trajectory. All of my earthly belongings now fit in a small pickup. I thought back to the house in Phoenix; it had a pool (nice, but not quite big enough), and four bedrooms (but why not five?). The other homes we'd owned over the years were also nice, but never quite nice enough. I never seemed to be satisfied. Why was this day so different?

I don't want to get too philosophical about it, but I believe my attention had been devoted to finding my identity by where I lived and what I drove. Did I wish I had a big screen TV instead a 22-inch one with a bad speaker in that little cottage? Sure. Would I get one? Maybe. But I also wouldn't be discontent if I waited five or ten years.

The Apostle Paul said, "I have learned to be content in whatever state I'm in." I was finally learning to be content. That day, I experienced a touch of contentment. I was at peace with what I owned and what I didn't. Admittedly, I have devoted a lot of time and energy to being bigger and better than others, but that day I felt like my climb up the ladder of success had been leaning against the wrong wall.

Life Lesson #48: Learn to be content. Be at peace with what you own and what you don't.

When I woke up the next morning, it was time to revisit Matthew 5, known as The Sermon on the Mount. Verse three says, "Blessed are the poor in spirit, for theirs is the kingdom of God." The emphasis is not placed on being financially poor, but rather being poor in spirit. It describes a man who has been beaten to his knees, who has nothing at all, yet puts his complete trust in God. We experience being poor in spirit when the pain of our circumstances and adversity beats us to our knees, and we come to God in humble submission. Short stints in jail, being homeless, the loss of a great family, friends and good jobs—the net result had left me poor in spirit.

William Barclay summed it up best: "Blessed is the man who has realized his own utter helplessness, and who has put his whole trust in God. He will be completely detached from things, for he will know that things have not got it in them to bring happiness or security; and he will become completely attached to God."

Because so few ever reach that rare place of detachment, we continue to hang on to our possessions and our high places in society, striving for more power and prestige. Is that why Jesus said, "It's easier for a camel to go through the eye of a needle than for a rich man to enter the kingdom of God?"

God's kingdom reigns now, just as it does in the next life. For a real alcoholic, our positions and possessions prove to be only a temporary fix; then we are back to the bottle and eventually placed in a grave or beaten to our knees in humble acceptance of our need for a Power greater than ourselves. There's nothing wrong with owning stuff; it's when our stuff owns us that things get lonely, even lethal.

I accepted the job in Mobile as a drug and alcohol counselor because I needed a job. In the initial interview with my soon-to-be boss, I felt like I was selling out. I compromised my core values in the name of becoming gainfully employed. After reviewing my resumé, my would-be supervisor walked behind her desk in a condescending, pompous manner. She was wound way too tightly, and she gave the appearance of being educated well beyond her actual intelligence.

She sounded like a Pharisee as she grilled me with a battery of questions. "Is it true that you used to be a pastor, Mr. Henderson?" she asked as she looked at me over the rim of her glasses.

"Yes, ma'am, I was," I answered. "That is, before I got kicked out for being a drunk." I said it with a calm sense of admission; I was neither ashamed nor proud of my past.

"I think that's fine," she continued. "I believe in God, but I want you to understand this is not a religious environment. Therefore, the subject of God is not to be brought up. Do you understand, Mr. Henderson?"

"I understand what you're saying, yes. However, I don't see myself as a wild-eyed evangelist who can't wait to lay hands on my clients and deliver them from their disorders." At this point, I became a little more jittery. "But on occasion, clients have requested prayer and I have been more than willing to oblige."

"Well, Mr. Henderson, if they make that request here, would you please ask them to see their rabbi, priest, pastor, or whoever? Anyone but you. Do you understand me, Mr. Henderson?"

"Yes, ma'am, I understand what you are saying perfectly." I knew how Simon Peter must have felt when he denied his identity with Christ.

The interrogation went on. "It has also been reported that you are a recovering alcoholic. Is that true, Mr. Henderson?"

"Yes, ma'am, I will soon be celebrating ten years of sobriety. Life has been good."

She told me she thought that was great. "My brother is a recovering alcoholic, and AA has been of great value to him. However, I want you to understand that this is not a Twelve Step program, and I will not have you bring up the name or say anything about AA. Is that clear?"

"Yes, ma'am, I understand."

The conversation made me feel like a hired prostitute, like I was being paid to conduct a service that I had no interest in, other than collecting the money for it. The two bedrock issues of my sobriety had been cut to the core. I felt like a butcher without a knife, or a soldier sent to battle without a weapon. But I made a concerted effort to honor our agreement, and most of the time, I was successful.

Six months went by while I worked like a singer without a voice. Then one day, I received a startling phone call while I was busy climbing my way out of the usual massive avalanche of paperwork. It was a job offer from a faith-based agency in Daphne, over on the east bay. It was less than ten minutes from my home, and I'd be able to speak openly about the things that I believed in. They said they were looking for a counselor who had the necessary academic requirements but was also able to offer their own life experiences as teaching tools.

This new job proved to be a rewarding position. It gave me an opportunity to reach clients through counseling and the Scriptures, and there was a real sense of satisfaction from knowing that helping those people could have a positive impact that extended for generations to come. The facility required clients to attend the church of their choosing. I thought I could start a weekly gathering, teaching the Scriptures to clients and anyone else who wanted to come.

We rented a local yacht club to use on Sunday mornings. I was allowed to invite any client of the facility who wanted to attend. I was excited. As a recovering drunk myself, it was a great feeling to explain the Bible to other recovering addicts.

A lot of people who came to the gatherings were seeking spirituality, but as recovering addicts they didn't feel at home in a traditional church setting. Clients would tell me how out of place they felt in a church; most average people didn't understand what it was like to be in recovery. They felt judged, condemned, and subtly ridiculed, as if they had a contagious disease that should be avoided at all costs.

We had music at our gatherings—some of the clients were gifted musicians and vocalists and for some of them, this was the first time they'd ever played before a crowd without being self-medicated with drugs or alcohol. They would tell me that the experience was definitely different, but they liked it. For some, it was the first time they had ever felt like they were part of a group that genuinely cared for them.

We were all on a journey together, and I didn't want it to end. However, like many things in life, it did end.

One summer day, I rode my Harley to Arkansas to see the kids. One was getting married; another was having a child; yet another was enrolled in college. I faced the grim realization that they were growing up, whether I was there or not. If I was going to be a part of their lives, I needed to be present. So, I made the decision to leave my sweet home in Alabama and move closer to my children.

When I got back to work after having been gone for two weeks, my supervisor informed me that the case load at our rehab facility had declined. Since I was the last one to be hired, I would be the first one fired. Little did he know that my heart had already moved back to Arkansas; I just needed to gather my belongings. I told my Sunday morning group that I needed my kids and my kids needed me, and I had to do what I felt was right. They were disappointed but seemed to understand.

One of the most memorable experiences while living in the Red Neck Riviera, as I called this part of the country, was riding up and down the beach from Gulf Shores to Pensacola. Usually the experience was liberating, and it made me feel like a kid every time—except on my last ride. Whatever had been beckoning me before seemed to be silent now. It felt like my time living there was up. Did I want the latter years of my life to be filled with fisherman reeling in sharks and sting rays and riding the highway at dusk, or time spent with my kids and grandchildren?

I knew what the answer was, without hesitation. I loaded up and headed back to Arkansas.

When I arrived there, I knew I'd made the right choice. I found a job about an hour away from the state line in a small town in Oklahoma, working at a mental health facility. Mental stability must begin with a clear understanding of who God is and the power of His strength in our life. It's not the cure-all for every issue, but it is the first step. Sometimes people would come to me humbly seeking hope beyond what their personal abilities or a counselor could offer. I felt in my heart if they only had a deeper understanding of God, his love and guidance, their lives would take on a new direction.

I mentioned this concern to my supervisor, and she gave me permission to start a study group as long we didn't meet at our facility and didn't use the agency's name as an endorsement. That sounded simple enough, so I agreed. Before long, I had a large variety of people coming to the group—heroin and meth addicts, alcoholics, and people battling different kinds of emotional issues.

It was a strange-looking crowd compared to what you might expect for a Sunday morning Bible study, but I loved them, and they knew it. They had a look of desperation in their eyes; they had tried so many other approaches to solving their problems, yet nothing had worked. Some were well-educated and well-dressed. Others looked like a poster child for the homeless, and many had wrinkled clothes and messy hair. We ate, laughed, studied, and joked together as a group. Everything was going great until a well-meaning coworker reported me to the CEO of the agency.

A meeting was called with the human resource administrator, the CEO, and me. The interrogation lasted for less than an hour. They informed me that they would have to dismiss me from my job for maintaining a dual relationship—my counseling and the Sunday morning Bible study group.

It had been reported that I'd purchased a tire for one of my clients, an elderly gentleman. I explained that Ralph wouldn't be able to make it to his doctor appointments without one, but that didn't seem to matter.

I was also questioned about helping another client pay a fine so that she could avoid going to jail and losing custody of her child. In my heart, I knew what I was doing was a violation according to the code of ethics for licensed professional counselors, but I had done it anyway.

Was I a pawn just being used by some manipulative people? Was I being played like a fiddle? Maybe, but my intuition said help them, so I did. There were other, similar accounts the administration apparently didn't know about because they weren't brought up. But my supervisors still had enough information to give me the boot. My ministry with the misfits had ended. The administrator offered to get someone to help me clean out my office, but I declined, telling them I had plenty of experience at it.

Perhaps I blended in so well with a band of misfits because in many ways I felt that I was just like them. I grew up with an alcoholic dad, without a mother, raised by my grandmother in a household of eight. Things had been challenging at times.

When I was a kid, I had been in the Boy Scouts for a while. After a meeting one night, the pack leader told me to not come back until I got a haircut. He'd said I didn't meet the standards of the type of boys they were grooming. I didn't have the courage to tell the him that we didn't have the money for a haircut, so I never went back. I definitely felt like a misfit. I often went to school wearing dirty jeans and hand-me-down rags. Whether it was true or not, I felt like all of other kids wore nice, clean clothes and had well-groomed haircuts. It felt like I was the only misfit.

Back then, it felt like everybody in our tiny community knew what my dad had done to my mother. Some people probably were aware of who I was and what my background was like; others didn't know, and still others didn't care. Real or unreal, I felt like a leper, as if I had created a monster in my mind and lived with the agony every time I walked down the street. On the inside, I was riddled with fear and insecurity. I was a misfit.

Later I discovered that alcohol helped me cover the feelings I had deep on the inside. Even now, being sober for so long, I still feel like a misfit of a different sort. A misfit with two master's degrees who was kicked out of my church for being a drunk. A divorced, convicted felon misfit with five DUIs. I had just been trying to fit in with a group of fellow misfits. And now it was time to add one more star by name: unemployed misfit.

But I kept my faith in God, and I was reminded that things would be all right in spite of not having a job. I have done things in the past that were wrong, and I was justifiably punished for the deeds, but this time I felt no shame.

We had been holding our group study in an empty building on the campus of a church. AA conducted meetings there in the evenings, but on Sundays the space was vacant. When the pastor found out that I had been fired, he gave me the boot also. I was sad that the group ended, not only because I had enjoyed it, but also because it had been helping people, and now it had been taken away.

It's so easy to get caught up in people's problems, even when they have nothing to do with us. This pastor couldn't cope with the idea of being caught up in anything remotely controversial, so he avoided the situation entirely. Apparently, he didn't like the idea of being associated with a rule breaker.

There was a time in my life when my brilliant reasoning would have told me that before I left the pastor's office, he needed his eye blackened and a window or two kicked out. Instead, I decided to leave his eye alone and just started looking for a job. Sometimes it's better to leave other people's issues alone and look for a solution instead.

Life Lesson #49: It's easy to get caught up in trying to

fix other people's problems. But it's often better to leave other people's issues alone and work on your own situation instead.

I was out of work for a few months. During that time, I took the opportunity to repaint my Harley and do some serious riding. Then a friend told me about a mental health agency in Miami, Oklahoma, that was hiring, so I made a call and scheduled an interview. I met with the young, friendly director named Beth, and was immediately offered a position.

Since I began AA in earnest, I have never hidden my past history of addiction; it is what it is. I would rather she find out now than be fired again later. So, I told Beth of my history with alcohol. She seemed pleased with my sobriety and honesty. She also mentioned they were in the process of negotiating a contract with the Department of Corrections, and they were looking for a counselor to assist in their rehab program. She asked me if I would be interested in working with people with addiction problems as well as clients with emotional issues.

I tried to keep my composure, so I just graciously said that I would be honored. On the inside, I was jumping with joy to work with a population of people I loved and respected.

The clientele assigned to me at my new position all had at least three felonies. The judge would offer them a deal to avoid prison if they were willing to get help for their addiction, and if they chose not to sign up, they would face anywhere from five to twenty years. Many addicts gladly signed up just to avoid hard time in prison.

I understood that most of them were more motivated to stay out prison than to stay clean, but that was ok with me. I probably would have taken the same offer even if I wasn't interested in finding a new way of life.

However, there are some clients who have a moment of clarity and make an internal decision to get off the downward-spiraling track and seek to be free from the bondage of alcohol and drugs. When I'm able to see that change taking place, it's one of the most rewarding experiences I've ever known. Not only does that clarity change their life, but also the lives of their spouse, children and maybe even grandchildren.

I kept that possibility in mind as I worked with these clients. Sometimes my efforts and faith paid off; at other times, not. But I kept moving forward, helping those I could.

Part of the community sentencing in the drug and alcohol program I've been involved with is aimed at allowing addicts to stay out of prison if they are willing to get help for their addiction. I was the therapist for Mayes County, so clients had to meet with me on a weekly basis for individual and group therapy sessions. They also had to stay clean, live in a drug-free environment, and have a job. For a while, I had a client who began repeatedly missing her scheduled appointments.

After being AWOL for several weeks, she finally wandered back in. In my gracious, loving style, I politely asked her where in the hell she had been. She gave me one of the lamest excuses I've heard—she couldn't find a ride. When I asked her why she didn't at least call, she told me she didn't have money for a cell phone.

Now, that seemed more plausible to me. Many of my clients lived on the edge of financial disaster. She told me how much a phone would cost, so I gave her the money to buy one and told her to call in if she was going to miss her appointment. She agreed. I thought the matter was dealt with, and it might even keep her from ultimately going to prison.

I knew the code of ethics for licensed professional counselors prohibited such deeds, but it seemed like the right thing to do at the time. Bending and sometimes breaking the rules is sometimes my style. I drive faster than the speed limit allows, and sometimes I get tickets. I have chosen to help other clients in the past, and they benefitted. My decision might have helped this particular client too; at least she got a phone.

However, the decision ended up harming me.

Several weeks passed, and we didn't hear from her. She was a no call, no show again. In our treatment team meeting, I recommended that she spend five days in the county jail as a form of shock treatment, with hopes of waking her up before she was revoked and sent to prison. The treatment team agreed.

When my client was informed of the consequences of her failure to make her appointments, she told the probation officer that she had not been attending scheduled sessions because she was afraid of me. She reported that I might even have romantic interests in her, as evidenced by the money I gave her for the phone. I was fired again.

When we make an effort to help others, we always run the risk of being used and manipulated. This time, I definitely felt used and manipulated, with much regret. Nothing is more rewarding than helping someone in their recovery, and nothing is more frustrating than being played. It seems to be a gamble every time.

For several months, I contemplated the possibility of just quitting counseling altogether. I figured it would be best to leave the gambling business behind and simply avoid working with others. Walmart could always use good greeter at the door. And somebody's got to flip those burgers—maybe I could get an employee discount on Big Macs.

I felt like working for the Department of Corrections in Community Sentencing had been the best job I had ever had. It seemed like I was following my calling. At this time, I was disillusioned about the whole system, disappointment with myself, and feeling like a failure. I told my girlfriend that I was going to quit this line of work. She told me, "Don't let that bitch win, Ron."

I wasn't convinced that I had the energy to get back in the ring and go a few more rounds, I was so tired and deflated. I was at retirement age so I looked into collecting my Social Security and drifting off into the sunset like an old cowboy that gave up riding bucking broncos. I would just wither away, build a little cabin, and isolate myself. Justifying it by declaring I had paid my dues, I hoped that my Lord would feel we were even now, and I didn't owe him anything—my debt had been paid. But in my heart I knew I wasn't being honest. For one thing, if I lived to be a thousand years old, I could never repay the good that had been disposed on my behalf. And furthermore, one of reasons I had been sober for almost two decades is because I have been able to help others in their quest to stay clean and sober.

For the next year I proceeded to plug along without a clear path of where I was going. Before I was fired, I had bought a large house on Grand Lake in northeast Oklahoma. It needed to be remodeled so all of my money and time was devoted to this project. I never started collecting Social Security, but I was running out of money. During this time I was fortunate enough to pick up a part time job that allowed me to pay most of my bills before services were cut off. It seemed as though God was just saying, "Hold on, be steady, and trust me, it will get better, things will different." I did as I was told.

IX

LISTEN WHEN THE SMALL
VOICE SPEAKS

I CONTINUED to go to AA meetings, and the support I received and gave others helped keep me sober, so I wasn't willing to change what had worked for me for so many years. I have heard it said that if something is working for you, don't change it. AA had consistently worked for me.

One particular night I really didn't feel like going to the meeting, but I went anyway. It was an eating meeting, where a guest speaker would share while we enjoyed a pot luck dinner. I had set my plate down next to some buddies and I went back to get my drink. I passed a middle-aged man who was sitting alone. I've one to receive a lot direct revelation from God through verbal messages, but in my spirit a voice seemed to be saying, Go back to man that man, maybe you can be an encouragement. I turned around while quietly grumbling to myself, and I sat down and introduced myself. After I told him a little bit about my drunken days as a Pastor, Al proceeded to share similar experiences as the music director at a church. We both chuckled with a little bit of shame and embarrassment.

In the course of our conversation I asked Al what he did for living at present. He told me he worked in the marketing department of a recovery facility in Jay, Oklahoma. I was impressed and told me of my background in counseling since I had been sober. Out of the blue, he then asked me if I wanted a job. I flashed him a big smile, gulped hard, and said yes!

I didn't tell him I was about 12 inches away from the welfare line, but I did go on to tell him my heart was committed to finishing out my final days working with addicts even though for the past year my faith had been shaken and tested, bombarded with doubt and fear that it might not happen.

Within a few weeks Janet Wilkerson, the CEO of Christian Alcoholics and Addicts in Recovery, (CAAIR), asked me if I wanted a job as a counselor. Once again the tide had turned! I used to believe that working for Community Sentencing was the best job I had ever had and would ever have, but I was wrong. The job with CAAIR is the best job that I have ever had. Working in a faith based, family oriented atmosphere is unparalleled. The 12 Steps of AA are strongly endorsed, and the clients are required to work as part of their recovery. Some of them have never been gainfully employed before, due to their addiction. The agency's holistic approach to helping others prepare for the future is unique. They focus on counseling in addition to helping clients get a legal driver's license as well as other things such as a birth certificate.

I recently told Mrs. Wilkerson that someday I wanted to have to have my funeral at the campus. What could be better? A room full of drunks and junkies, my kids, grandkids, and a few friends.

Although my faith was tested, God has shown himself to be faithful in His love for me once again.

I often tell my clients, "I know you're feeling beat up and bedraggled, squeezed and stomped, but just don't give up, the tide will turn." We sometimes make the error of believing our problems will always be with us, but if our faith is put in a power greater than ourselves and we hang in and hang on, things will get better.

I am reminded of Proverbs 3:5-6: "Trust in the Lord with all thine heart and do not lean on thine own understanding; In all thy ways acknowledge him, and he shall direct thy paths." Invariably, things get shaky when I start leaning on my own understanding in the absence of my creator's guidance.

It is easy for to trust the Lord on sunny days when everything is working in our favor, but when we drift down the path of darkness and fear the doubts begin to emerge. I hadn't totally accepted the fact that I would finish out the last two minutes of the game of life sitting on the bench but I had no evidence that it would be different other than what He promised in His word and what He planted in my heart. I had been engulfed with doubts, but working with criminals, junkies, and drunks is what I long to do until I finish the last lap of life.

As we try to figure out how life works, it's important to remember that we should avoid doubting in the dark what God has promised to us in the light.

Life Lesson #50: Don't doubt in the dark what God has promised us in the light.

X

LOOKING BACK WITH
NEW PERSPECTIVE

SEVERAL YEARS AGO, I was having lunch with a friend in Gulf Shores, and he asked me if I thought God leads us down the pathways of addiction to make us stronger. I told him that my mistakes and bad choices were all self-inflicted, and that I couldn't give God credit for the depth of my own stupidity.

Then I wadded up my napkin and threw it on the floor. I said, "If I leave it laying where it is, eventually a janitor will come by, sweep it up, and dispose of it with the rest of the trash. That's where my life was a few years ago. I would have been disposed of, like so many others. Instead, God reached down and picked me up."

I picked up my napkin and said, "Here I am today. I'm wrinkled, soiled, and scarred, but willing to be used. Left to my own devices, I would have been buried at the dump to decompose. God picked me up off of the floor, but he didn't place me there."

Life Lesson #51: Much of our pain, suffering and bad choices has been self- inflicted; we can't give God credit or blame for the depth of our stupidity.

RECENTLY, I celebrated eighteen years of sobriety.

Now that I have a panoramic view of my life, I can see more clearly the big picture. Growing up with an alcoholic father and no mother left some deep scars on my soul. After my spiritual awakening at eighteen, the ragged edges of my life began smoothing out, and life finally began to make sense.

From that point on, all I wanted to do was tell others about the wonderful message of God's grace and love. I started out on a mission to find just one other young man who was equally as emotionally disturbed and spiritually disjointed as I had been, so I could share with him the wonderful freedom I'd experienced.

Somewhere in my quest, I made the wrong turn. And it has taken years of self-examination, struggle, poor decisions, and pain to make it back to a place of balance.

Wherever we are in life, we are there because of choices we have made, good or bad. That's not to say there haven't been caring people who have helped us, and a loving God who has strengthened us. But we are responsible for the choices we make, and the consequences of those choices.

An elder in my church in Phoenix once told me he had me figured out—I was a maverick. Maybe it was not intended to be a compliment or an insult, just an observation. Webster's Dictionary defines maverick this way:

1.An unbranded range animal.

2.An independent individual who does not go along with a group or party.

Independence is a good thing, when used wisely. It is important that we don't become herd animals that just blindly follow the group. Diversity is necessary to keep our planet balanced, so celebrate your uniqueness, and enjoy the commonalities you have with others. Live without compromise and embrace your core values.

But always remember, being a maverick doesn't mean living a life without God. And if all you do is go your own way into addiction, your independence isn't serving you well.

As I reflect back now, I realize that the process of formulating my thoughts on life began about ten years ago—I've essentially been writing this story, in one way or another, for years. A lot has happened over the years, but the same two themes continue to reemerge in my writings over the years: We are the captain of our ship, and the rudder is in our control. We live and die by our thoughts and actions. The responsibility is ours.

Life Lesson #52: You are the captain of your ship; the rudder is under your control. You will live and die by your thoughts and actions, as they dictate your destination.

CONCLUSION

MY VIEW of my place in the world has changed too. When I was in college, I got my pilot's license while all of my buddies were studying the Greek language, the original language of the New Testament. Back in those days, I thought I would need to fly all over the country because I would be in such high demand. Millions of people would want to hear me pontificate on great truths. I am pretty sure that I was just motivated by selfish ambition. The only place I ended up flying to was the county jail. That seems to be the destination for many who are driven by alcohol and pride.

———

Today, my expectations have lessened and become more grounded in reality. Traveling on my bike is important as long as health allows. Being a good father and grandfather is the best job a man can ever have. Occasionally, I dream about taking a cruise with a beautiful woman, having my arm around her as we gaze out on the ocean at dusk. Lofty ideas about taking my show nationwide and becoming famous are no longer on my bucket list.

———

Another thing I've come to realize is that we must be self-aware if we want to be healthy. In group therapy, we acknowledge that drugs and alcohol had a positive effect on some level, or we wouldn't have paid such a great price to abuse them. When I ask what the benefits are of using and abusing, the common response is that it makes the user feel confident and bolder—he feels less inhibited when interacting with others (especially with the ladies).

———

When I first got sober, I asked myself the same question. Memory took me back to the thirteen-year-old kid who was filled with a thousand forms of insecurity and fear. Alcohol made me better-looking, the women always looked better, and I was bigger and badder. It just took cheap whiskey to create that formula.

———

I made the decision early on in my sobriety to duplicate this attitude toward life—such as being an extrovert, being bolder and more confident—only I would do so without using alcohol. At first, it was awkward and scary to act as though I had those qualities. But I practiced the art of being less inhibited and more outgoing until it came naturally and normally.

———

Not long ago, my daughter Megan told her seven-year-old daughter, Addison, that her "Silly Grandpa" had just celebrated seventeen years of sobriety. Addison looked puzzled. Megan asked if she knew what that meant, and Addison simply said, "No, I don't know what you're talking about."

———

Megan explained that it had been seventeen years since Silly Grandpa had drunk any alcohol. In her young, undeveloped mind, what Addison heard her mom say was, "Grandpa has been drinking alcohol for seventeen years."

———

Addison said, "Oh, I get it, so that's why he acts that way."

———

When I heard this story, I was so happy! My strategy of over-coming fear and introversion is working—without alcohol. Being sober entails living a life of contentment and inner peace that alcohol could never offer.

———

I didn't know if this approach was really working, though, until I was at a large family gathering not long ago. There were about fifty people there, and I was one of only a few guests not drinking. But I was having fun anyway.

———

A friend of my daughter saw my bold behavior and asked if I had been drinking. Megan told her friend, "No, my dad always acts that way."

———

The only difference is, I do it without alcohol. And I'm better off for it.

———

I'll close with Eight Bedrock Beliefs, core values; principal characteristics that have help hold me together when everything else was coming apart.

Eight Bedrock Beliefs
From *Memoirs of Drunken Preacher*

1. I know I am weak; God loves me unconditionally and empowers me to succeed beyond my wildest expectations.
2. Embrace core values, cling to your uniqueness. Don't let the world squeeze you into its mold.
3. Dream big. Taking calculated risks is essential for a full life.
4. Push yourself to the limit, demand of yourself all that you have. We all have unbelievable talents that are not being fully utilized.
5. Persistence allows us to excel beyond others with far more talent. Don't ever give up in the midst of difficulty.
6. If possible, find humor in the midst of pain, don't take yourself so seriously. Laughter is one of the biggest joys of life.
7. Let go of resentments and hate. Focus on what we have gained from the past and the hand that we were dealt.
8. Absorb yourself in the success of others, and in the end you will be successful.

ABOUT THE AUTHOR

Ron is a Licensed Professional Counselor for Christian Alcoholics and Addicts in Recovery in Jay, Oklahoma. The author has earned a Masters of Arts Degree from Dallas Theological Seminary and a Masters of Science Degree from John Brown University in Siloam Springs, Arkansas.

In addition to riding motorcycles and restoring classic cars, Ron also speaks at churches and self help groups, telling his story of hope and encouragement.

For more information, visit www.drunkenpreacher.com

39521429R00124

Made in the USA
Lexington, KY
19 May 2019